if you're clueless about selling

and want to know more

SETH GODIN

Dearborn
Financial Publishing, Inc.

D1318904

If You're Clueless about Selling and Want to Know More

Editorial Director: Cynthia A. Zigmund
Managing Editor: Jack Kiburz
Interior and Cover Design: Karen Engelmann

© 1998 by Seth Godin Productions, Inc.

Published by Dearborn Financial Publishing, Inc.¨®

Printed in the United States of America
98 99 00 10 9 8 7 6 5 4 3 2 1

Library of Congress Cataloging-in-Publication Data
Godin, Seth.
    If you're clueless about selling and want to know more / Seth Godin
            p.   cm.
    Includes index.
    ISBN 0-7931-2989-3 (pbk.)
    1. Selling.   I. Title.
    HF5438.25.G633   1998
    658.85–dc21   98-30389
                                                           CIP

Dearborn books are available at special quantity discounts to use as premiums and sales promotions, or for use in corporate training programs. For more information, please call the Special Sales Manager at 800-621-9621, ext. 4384, or write to Dearborn Financial Publishing, Inc., 155 North Wacker Drive, Chicago, IL 60606-1719.

Other Clueless books by Seth Godin:

If You're Clueless about Mutual Funds and Want to Know More

If You're Clueless about Retirement Planning and Want to Know More

If You're Clueless about Saving Money and Want to Know More

If You're Clueless about the Stock Market and Want to Know More

If You're Clueless about Insurance and Want to Know More

If You're Clueless about Starting Your Own Business and Want to Know More

If You're Clueless about Accounting and Finance and Want to Know More
(with Paul Lim)

If You're Clueless about Getting a Great Job and Want to Know More
(with Beth Burns)

If You're Clueless about Financial Planning and Want to Know More
(with John Parmelee)

Acknowledgments

Thanks to Jack Kiburz and Cynthia Zigmund at Dearborn for their invaluable editorial guidance; Karen Watts, who created the Clueless concept; and Laura Spinale who pulled it all together.

Thanks, too, to the crew at SGP for their never-ending insight and hard work.

Contents

GETTING
a
Clue
about
SELLING

Everybody's a salesman— from the professional real estate agent who hands you the keys to your new home, to the small-business owner trying to garner new clients, to the corporate employee lobbying his boss for a raise.

You need to sell. Selling is the pulse of every business. Without sales, there is no business.

You may be the owner of a small company that offers its clients a terrific, A-1, absolutely wonderful service. But if you can't sell it—if you can't prospect, get appointments, uncover your clients' needs, and link your service to those needs— you'll declare Chapter 11 inside a year.

Or you may work as an accountant with a large firm. You're the top guy, the one the

firm's clients scramble for. But if you can't link the value of your services to your employer's needs, you'll never get that much-deserved raise, or make partner.

Perhaps you've even thought about forging a career in sales itself, but you don't know how. Or, as a new salesman, you think you know how, but you're not making the money you want.

Don't fret. Selling is a skill. Like any skill—from skiing to brain surgery—it requires the mastery of certain techniques. And, despite the pervasive myth of the "natural-born salesman," these techniques can be learned. This book will teach you the most important.

Absorbing these techniques, practicing them so they become second nature, will take more than a little effort on your part. But the good news is this: A great salesman can always make a great living, whether he chooses to sell computers or newspaper advertising, pianos or web TV. Your investment of time gets paid back in cash.

And, unlike many other occupations, sales will never bore you.

Who do you want to be today? Your choices include psychologist, entertainer, reporter, efficiency expert, image maker, or P.R. maven. If you can't pick just one, that's OK. There's really no reason why you should have to.

A successful sales career combines all these occupations. Use psychology to understand a buyer's body language. Don a reporter's hat to prospect for new clients. Enjoy the spotlight when you show off your wares. Build a client's image when you sell him a product that enhances his status in his community, and become an efficiency expert as you tout products that help businesses run more smoothly.

Learning all these skills may sound impossible to you, but it's not. And regardless of whether your realize it, you probably sell already.

Read this book, and here's what you'll learn:

- *Learning the Lingo and the Mechanics*
  Study the sales jargon that will make you sound like an insider from your

The Natural-Born Ichthyologist? (Debunking the Myth of the "Natural-Born Salesman")

Let's talk, for a minute, about the fish guy—aka the ichthyologist. His name is Jack. He's the best fish guy in the business. Nobody understands the fish mind the way Jack does. The Nobel committee, off in Sweden, has developed a new category, "For Extraordinary Research in the Field of Salmon," just to pay him homage.

His mother sits at home, drinking coffee with her friends, basking in her son's moment, saying, "You know, ever since he was a little boy, his dad and I knew, absolutely knew, that Jack would become an ichthyologist. He just always seemed to have a fish personality."

Baloney.

Jack, at some point in his life, developed an affinity for fish. That affinity led him to study the species, to work hard to develop certain skills. Only then did he become the ultimate fish guy.

No one is a natural-born salesman.

Some of your friends and acquaintances may seem naturally more outgoing than you. They may better "connect" with people than you.

There's no such thing as a natural-born ichthyologist.

And there's no such thing as a natural-born salesman.

Have no fear. Selling is a skill. And like every skill, it can be learned. Natural bents count for little. Honed sales skills count for everything.

first day at the office. Learn the inner workings of every successful sale, from prospecting to customer care.

- *To Market, to Market*
  Brochures and advertisements don't sell, you do! Still, you need to know how your company has positioned its product in the market—the highest-tech gadget in the industry, the low-cost leader, the durable choice—then tailor your plug to meet the needs of individual prospects. There's a section for those trying to learn how to position their goods.

- *Digging for Gold: Targeting Your Prospects*
  You can't sell to everyone. You don't want to sell to everyone. You'll only waste your time and energy. Instead, learn through referrals and other prospecting techniques how to find the prospects who truly need your wares.

- *Getting an Appointment*
  In any family or organization there is a person or a group that boasts both the desire for your product and the means to pay for it. Nobody else matters too much, and you'll waste a lot of time if you insist on selling to those who can only say "no." In this chapter, you'll learn how to find the Yes Guy, and study cold-calling techniques that will help you get in the door for a presentation.

- *First Impressions*
  The first impression isn't just about looking sharp when you walk in the door for your presentation. Your client forms his initial impression of you from earlier active and passive contacts, including your reputation in the community, the cadence of your voice during cold calls, and other factors. Learn how to make a great first impression every step of the way.

- *Asking Questions*
  Don't assume you know what your prospect wants or needs. You must ask strategic questions to uncover what she really cares about.

- *The Presentation*
  Like sales itself, most presentations follow a certain formula: Business-based small talk leads to strategic questioning, leads to linking your wares to your prospect's needs, leads to overcoming objections and then to closing. Learn the process.

- *The Push*
  No matter how well you've done your homework, no matter how well you've linked your goods to your prospect's needs, your prospect, like all humans, suffers from an inherent fear of saying "yes." Learn, through closing techniques, how to help him overcome that fear.

- *Keeping the Sale and Generating Repeat Business*
  Your work isn't finished once the prospect signs a contract. Follow-ups and customer care lead to repeat business, and help generate referrals.

- *Making a Career in Sales*
  Learn the attitude, time, management techniques, and marketing skills that will help you get up and sell every morning, even during inevitable periods of slump.

- *The Sale*
  Read some soup-to-nuts scenarios covering the entire sales process, from prospecting to customer care.

But before you hone any of these techniques, you need to get yourself into the enthusiastic mind-set that leads to sales.

Let's start there.

Your Attitude

When are you more nervous—when asking for a favor or when offering a favor?

Do you feel more comfortable when you say to a friend or acquaintance, "Umm, my car is in the shop, and I was wondering if you wouldn't mind too much giving me a

ride to the party on Saturday?" Or when you say to the same pal, "Look, I heard your car is in the shop. How about I give you a ride to the party?"

It's easier to offer help than to ask for help. You feel more confident lending a hand than accepting one.

Keep this psychological phenomenon in mind from the first day of your sales career.

Confidence is the salesman's most valuable asset. But many, many people new to the field don't feel confident—they feel, well, fearful.

Why?

They think this:

"During every cold call, during every presentation, during every close, I'm asking for a favor. I'm asking someone for the favor of buying my product."

Stop that kind of self-talk right now.

Instead, think this:

"I believe I can help every prospect I call. I've done my research, and I'm not contacting anyone willy-nilly. These are people who truly need my service, and I'm going to do my best to help them."

This attitude will immediately reduce your fear and help put you in the self-confident mind-set necessary to succeed in sales.

But you can't look upon this attitude as a mental gimmick. You can't keep saying to yourself, "I truly believe I can help every prospect upon whom I call," then go try to peddle your organic cat food to the local kennel club. You can't think, "My services will help Martin Industries reduce overtime costs by 20 percent," if you have chosen to ally yourself with a cut-rate company, one whose service contracts contain a veritable spider web of hidden costs and obligations.

Help each prospect by representing a company you respect, by selling a product you

You Can't Fake Integrity

Your integrity should pervade every step of the sales process. Because your prospects will instinctively pick up on any shadiness. It will scare them. And scared prospects won't buy.

How do you build your integrity?

- Represent only products you believe in.

- Call only on those prospects who need your product or service.

- Don't try to increase your commission by touting contracts with hidden features or hidden costs.

- Be up-front about the services and obligations included in your contract.

- Walk away if you find you truly can't help a prospect.

Finally, beware of using proprietary information. When you deliver a presentation to a prospect, talk about clients you have helped, comparing their needs with your prospect's. This is a valuable sales tool, but be careful not to say too much without permission.

Suppose your prospect and client compete in the same industry. You can't tell your prospect, "Until they got our software, Mr. Jones's staff was really inefficient. Because of that, they put together a less-than-great proposal to Masters Communications and almost lost them as a client."

Tell your prospect this, and—it's only human nature—the minute you leave the office he will call Masters Communications. And he may well wrest future contracts away from your Mr. Jones.

You've not only harmed an existing client, but you've probably irreparably damaged your chances of selling your prospect. He's not going to want you to know anything about his operations now, because he'll fear you'll blab to his competitors.

trust, and by developing prospecting skills so that you only call upon those with a legitimate need for your product or service.

It boils down to integrity.

Building Rapport and Trust

All the integrity and confidence in the world won't propel you to a successful sales career if you can't relate those qualities to your prospect. With each potential client, you need to take some time building rapport and trust.

Here's how:

- View prospects as new acquaintances you want to help. "Acquaintance" is the key word here, not "friend." Especially early in your relationship with a prospect or client, you need to follow conventional social protocol.

Whether at cocktail parties or during sales presentations, people get to know each other by slow degrees.

Think of it this way. Suppose you ran into your boss's husband in the office parking lot. You've met him once or twice at holiday parties and other professional functions. He's standing there, looking under the hood of his car, shaking his head. It appears to you that he needs a jump, and is wondering whether he has his cables.

How are you going to approach this acquaintance?

Are you going to say, clapping him on the back, "Hey, Bobby, how the hell are ya? Uh ooh—looks like somebody needs a jump. What, you left the cables in the basement? That's the right place for 'em, Bobby, the right place. But don't worry, pal—I got mine. I'll give you a jump."

You might joke around this way with your oldest, dearest friend, but certainly not with the boss's husband. Instead, simple etiquette demands that you approach the gentleman saying something like, "Hello, Mr. Carson, remember me? Wes, from the office Christmas party? Can I give you a hand here? I have some jumper cables in my trunk."

How to Tell if You Believe in Your Product

You can't expect a prospect to believe in your product if you don't. This is the first rule of sales. Your prospect will pick up on your distrust and make it his own. A prospect who doesn't trust a salesman or product won't invest.

How can you tell if you believe in your product?

The first question you ask yourself is: Would I buy it?

Put yourself in a prospect's shoes.

You sell heavy equipment to custom-home builders. Now, you and your family probably have no real need for, say, a derrick. So if you simply ask yourself, "Would I buy this derrick?" the answer will be, "No. Why would I?"

Instead, phrase the question this way: "If I were the owner of a custom-home construction company, would I buy this piece of equipment? Does it live up to the promises touted in sales brochures? Will it last? Is it capable of moving the amount of dirt I'd need to move?"

Here is a list of some questions to ask yourself to discover if you believe in your product and company:

- Would I buy it?

- Is it reasonably priced for the value it provides?

- Does it live up to the claims made in its advertising?

- Is the company I represent reputable, or do I sometimes get the feeling that it employs unpalatable sales tactics?

If for any reason you believe that your product, service, or company is less than reputable, you may want to consider switching jobs. A job change is always stressful, but it will prove worth it as your sales increase with your confidence in your wares.

As you get to know your clients better, a natural, more personal rapport may well begin to develop. That's fine, and right, and good. But at first, observe the same social niceties, allow the same social "space," you would with any new acquaintance, including your boss's husband.

- Learn to listen effectively. Later in the book, we'll talk about the importance of effective listening and questioning as a sales tool. There is no better way to build rapport with someone than to actually listen to him. Few people have learned this skill.

People hear all the time—they hear the background noise of another's concerns while their own minds race ahead toward the meeting at the end of the day, plans for the weekend, or stresses at home.

When you meet a prospect, truly listen to what she has to say. Clear your mind of other concerns. Look her in the eye. (It's more difficult for your mind to wander when you look someone in the eye.) Let her speak, but, when you don't understand something she's said, ask for clarification or elaboration. These requests will show her you've been paying attention.

Your prospect will welcome your interest. In fact, she'll feel flattered by it.

- The salesperson with the inside scoop knows the ins and outs of her industry. If you sell to consumers, study your community. Read industry magazines and local newspapers. Attend speeches given by those known to have the "inside scoop" on what's going on in your field. And then, when appropriate, share this information with your clients.

Send a magazine clipping to a client or prospect, or give him a buzz to tell him about a new move in the industry; it's a terrific move when you're trying to close a sale.

It's even more psychologically effective after he has signed a contract. It says you're in this relationship for the long haul.

When you take the time to clip a piece from an industry newspaper and send it to a client with a note saying, "Tom—I thought you might like to read about how ABC

Major Appliance's merger with Majapp USA will affect individual retailers. We'll talk soon about how to handle the changes," he'll know you care about the continued success of his business.

Be smarter, or at least better read, than your prospects and clients. Provide them with information they would not have received on their own. Then you become the guy with the inside scoop—not only a salesman, but a reference person. And you'll garner more sales by becoming a trusted source of information, a trusted ear, than by closing the sale and writing off the client.

But don't think that by sending an existing client a news clipping on Wednesday, you'll close a new sale on Friday. It's not that simple. By serving as a reference person as well as a salesman, you will eventually garner repeat sales. Eventually. You build for the long term.

And, the long-term view is the only view.

- Sell solutions. Of course, you could choose to peddle products. You could live your life as a barker touting the attributes of the latest snake oil.

Even if you sell a miracle baldness cure-all, you need to understand why your prospect wants hair.

Hair can be a pain in the neck. You must cut it, style it, buy shampoo and conditioner and mousse.

Uncover your prospect's hidden needs, and tout your product as a solution to those needs. Why does your client want hair? Don't assume that everyone necessarily wants it.

Listen to your client. Ask probing questions. Help him express his concerns.

He may say, "You know, I started shaving my head after I found my bald spot growing and growing. I decided just to be rid of hair for good. And I like being bald. I've saved $200 a year on hair-care products. And during the summer, when everyone else is sweating under a mass of curls, I feel cooler and freer. My wife thinks I look like

Captain Picard. The only problem is…being bald makes me look older. And older men in my company get shown the door more quickly than the younger guys."

Your prospect's problem is this: He's afraid that his premature baldness makes him look old. And old means "early retirement," which he doesn't want.

How do you respond?

"Mr. Smith, unfortunately, I think you're right. Baldness does make people look older, and, despite equality laws, large corporations would sooner retire well-paid senior executives than talented, less well paid younger employees. But I can help you. Our Hair Oil No. 3 has been scientifically proven to regrow hair within six weeks."

There is a distinct difference between touting your product as an amalgam of features and presenting it as a solution to your prospect's problem.

Your prospect doesn't want to buy another widget. He wants solutions. Sell the solution, and you'll make a successful career in sales.

- *Believe in your wares.* Your prospect will never, ever fall in love with your product if you've fallen out. Your prospect won't trust your company if you don't. Ally yourself with a product that excites you and a company with business practices you respect.

- *Arouse positive emotions.* Some words evoke fear, others enthusiasm. "Sell" will leave your prospect gripping his wallet, "help" will put him at his ease. "Buy" invokes fear, "invested in" brings to mind the American ideal of spending now for a future payoff.

- *Know the real person behind the professional mask.* Pick up on your prospect's body signals. If he sits behind the desk, with his hands placed over his head, he may be feeling "above" your wares or services. If he leans forward in his chair, listens to your pitch, nods, and says "OK," "Hey," or "Terrific!" he is indicating his willingness to buy, or at least listen to more of what you have to say. If you and your prospect have enjoyed the presentation, but, when it comes time to close, he fails to look you in the eye, and his objections to your wares keep shifting, you may be dealing with someone unable to give you a "yes."

Understanding your prospect's body language can help you decipher what he's feeling. Once you know what he feels, you can overcome unspoken objections and advance the sale. For more information, see chapter 10.

LEARNING *the* Lingo *and the* MECHANICS

CHAPTER TWO

After qualifying the prospect but before closing the sale, you'll probably have to ask a number of obligating questions.

Eyes starting to glaze over yet?

If you've just begun a career in sales, the first sentence of this chapter may seem to make little sense. Take heart: Every business boasts its own lingo, and you can learn sales jargon with about three minutes' study.

Be careful, though: You can use all the sales words you want when gathered around the water cooler in your office, swapping war stories with your colleagues. But you should not use them when talking with a prospect or customer. Saying, "Well, Pete, since your brother, Gus, told me you're in the market for a new car, I know you're a

pretty qualified lead," or "OK, Christine, it's time for me to ask a couple of obligating questions," will engender fear in your prospect. She won't really know what you're talking about, and she won't want to appear stupid.

Here's a list of sales words you should know:

- *Qualified leads* are people or companies you know both need and can pay for your offering.

- *Targeting of prospecting* is the process of developing a list of qualified leads—companies or individuals likely to buy your product or service.

- *Prospects* are whittled from a list of qualified leads; they are persons or companies you actively work to sell your product to.

- *Cold calling* is telephoning a prospect with the aim of securing a face-to-face meeting for your presentation.

- *Gatekeepers* are secretaries, executive assistants, security guards, voice-mail systems, or any other barrier that keeps salespeople from speaking directly to the Yes Guy.

- The *Yes Guy* is sometimes also called the "decision maker." The Yes Guy is the person in an organization or family who has both a desire for your product or service and the authority to OK the purchase. Sometimes the Yes Guy is an individual, sometimes an entire board or buying group.

- A *presentation/demonstration* is a face-to-face meeting with the Yes Guy to try to secure a contract for your product or service.

- *Tie downs* are statements the salesperson turns into questions to make discussions with clients feel conversational: "From what you've told me, Rob, you're quite concerned about alleviating your need for overtime during peak work seasons, isn't that true?" "Marian, isn't it accurate to say that your primary business concern is getting packages delivered on time, for a reasonable price?"

- *Advancement* is any step taken to bring you closer to an actual sale, such as the step from cold calling to a face-to-face presentation, the step from face-to-face presentation to answering a prospect's objections, the step from answering objections to closing.

- *Objections* are all the reasons a prospect gives for not buying your product or service. Common objections include: "We can't afford it." "I'll think about it." " I need to get some other quotes." As a salesman, you need to learn how to handle your prospect's objections to advance the sale.

- *Obligating questions* are an aid toward advancing, or closing, the sale. Obligating questions constitute a promise made if the prospect agrees to buy upon its fulfillment. Here's an example:

  Martin: "Look, I understand that you guys make terrific party supplies, and I'd love to have them in my novelty store. But the fact of the matter is, Halloween's just a month away, and I'm more concerned with getting 250 Batman and Superman masks in by next weekend."

  You: "If I can have those 250 masks in your store by next weekend, will you agree to contract with PartyLine as your primary supplier?"

- *Closing* is the process through which a prospect agrees to buy your product or service.

- *Closes* are techniques leading the customer to buy your product or service.

- *Referrals* are qualified leads given to you by a satisfied customer.

- *Follow-ups* or *customer care* are contacts with your customer after he has bought your product or service. You follow up to ensure that your product is working as it should, or to alleviate any problems your customer may have with it. Follow-ups and customer care not only serve as a measure of your caring professionalism, but often lead to repeat business.

- *Commission:* The fun part. This is the money your boss gives you for each sale completed. The amount is usually based on a percentage of the product's sale price.

Sales Mechanics

If you feel thirsty and want some water…well, you'll probably just head to the tap. But if you wanted to, you could visit your nearest laboratory. Combine two parts hydrogen with one part oxygen, and voilà!

H_2O is a proven scientific formula. It works every single time. You will never, ever combine two parts hydrogen with one part oxygen and get peanut butter, or corduroy, or cotton.

A single formula sits at the heart of every sale, and you need to understand its inner workings as well as the scientist understands his.

The scientist has an easier job of it than you do. Elements don't have personalities. They never yell at the scientist after a bad day in the beaker. They don't think about how to boost the laboratory's bottom line. And the scientist doesn't have to explain to hydrogen and oxygen how much more meaningful their lives will be if they will only combine to form water.

Sales is part science, part art. While the following formula sits at the heart of every sale, you need to tailor each step within it to suit an individual prospect's needs and personality. Otherwise, combine all these sales elements and you may end up not with a contract but with peanut butter, or cotton, or nothing.

Here's the formula:

- Obtain knowledge: Learn about your product or service, your company, your competition, your industry, and your prospect.

- Target your prospect: Generate lists of qualified leads using everything from cross directories to Securities and Exchange Reports, from local newspapers to the rosters of social organizations.

SKUs, MajAps, and ROM, Oh My!

While you don't want to use sales lingo in front of your customer, you should spend some time getting acquainted with the prospect's lingo.

Sell to the computer industry? You want to know that ROM stands for "read-only memory." Work with retailers? SKUs are "stock keeping units." If you represent a company that manufactures a revolutionary type of clothes dryer, you need to know that major appliances are often referred to as "MajAps."

Natural and appropriate use and understanding of your customer's lingo shows that you are a pro—an industry insider, a salesman who truly knows his stuff.

Suppose you've secured a major presentation to Home Trolley, a mammoth home improvement chain. You represent a company that has developed a new type of circular saw. The buyer likes your product a lot, but wants to know if your company has taken any steps to help retailers combat shrinkage.

Clearly, you don't want to reply: "Oh, no. It doesn't shrink at all, no matter how wet it gets. It might rust, but it won't shrink."

Imagine the look on the buyer's face.

You need to know that in the retail field, shrinkage is anything that contributes to a loss of inventory—from shoplifting to products breaking while on display.

Learning the customer's lingo will take some study on your part. Peruse industry trade magazines to get a feel for it. You can also ask people who won't think you're stupid for not knowing this jargon off the top of your head. It's OK to ask a more experienced salesperson in your company what "shrinkage" means. It's not appropriate to ask the prospect.

- Find the Yes Guy: Whether you sell to large corporations or families of four, uncover the person who has both the need for your product and the authority to pay for it.

- Get an appointment: Develop cold-calling techniques that will get you in the door to meet, face-to-face, with the Yes Guy.

- Plan your presentation: Use your research skills to learn as much specific information as you can about the prospect and his needs. Tailor your presentation to show how your product or service can help fulfill those needs.

- Present your goods or services: During a face-to-face meeting, use strategic questioning to help your prospect define his business needs. Explain how your product can fulfill those needs.

- Close: Reach an agreement with the customer wherein he decides he wants to buy your product or service, and you want to sell it to him.

- Generate referrals: Encourage satisfied customers to refer you to others who need your product or service.

- Follow up: Check back with your customer after he has purchased your product to make sure it is performing to his satisfaction.

The rest of this book offers in-depth discussions on these mechanics.

TO Market, to MARKET

CHAPTER THREE

Are you a small-business owner trying to determine how to position your product or service in the market? Or are you a member of a sales force trying to understand how the company you work for has decided to position its products?

The two situations are not quite as different as they first appear.

As a business owner, you may have taken on for yourself the responsibility of launching a sound marketing campaign, trying to find a niche that will garner the best return for your advertising dollars. As an employee, you need to understand how your wares have been positioned, to comprehend your client's likely perception of these products.

Building the Position

If you are now trying to find a marketing niche, remember this: Depending on your product, you may only waste money if you try to reach everybody.

Car manufacturers spend megabucks on network advertising because they want to reach everybody. And rightly so—the desire for a car cuts across all classes of Americans.

But your product probably has a much more narrow appeal. Not everyone needs or wants it.

Try to find the advertising venue that specifically targets the audience you wish to serve.

A diamond dealer will see a better return from consistent display ads on the "Engagements" page of his local newspaper than from a full-page layout in a regional magazine, or a commercial on radio or television, or on a Web page.

Why?

The latter choices reach too large an audience. People may read through the regional magazine for any number of reasons: They want to find out what movies are playing at what theaters. They want to learn how to best cultivate the roses that grow so well in your climate. They want to decorate their homes in the same manner as Mrs. High Society.

The engagement page of your local newspaper is read by the fiancées themselves, who may or may not have yet purchased a ring. It's also read by their families and their friends. Most of their friends are probably also reaching marrying age.

Sit down and study a bunch of different advertising venues to determine which will prove the best return for your dollar. Then decide how to position your product.

Your niche should prove neither too broad, nor too narrow.

Suppose you run your own pet-sitting business, and you are especially knowledgeable about and interested in caring for reptiles. A phrase like "We Sit for Your Pets" is too broad an advertising slogan because it doesn't target the reptile-owning population you hope to reach. Potential customers may think: "Sure, this guy can handle my dog and my cat, but can he deal with my iguana?"

But don't go to the other extreme. Don't advertise "We Sit for Your Pythons." Chances are, too few python owners live in your service area to make your business profitable.

"We Sit for Your Reptiles" perhaps serves as the best slogan. Neither too inclusive nor too exclusive, it will likely "hit" the customers you want to serve, letting them know that you specialize in caring for snakes, lizards, iguanas, and the like.

Understanding the Position

Your company has decided to position its products in a certain manner through advertising. Perhaps the company touts its wares as a lower-cost alternative, the durable choice, or the highest-tech gadget on the market. Advertising may also concentrate on the company's overall reputation as the business that truly cares for its clients.

Advertising venues include brochures, product catalogs, television and radio spots, and newspaper and magazine ads. Your company can also launch public relations efforts such as writing columns for newspapers; penning press releases detailing new products, and contributing to "Who's Come Aboard" and "Who's Been Promoted" columns.

Understanding the Perception

Study your company's advertisements and any press it has received to determine how your prospects are likely to perceive your product. These perceptions may determine whether a prospect will welcome you into his home or office for a presentation.

Let's say you represent a boutique wallpaper store. Its claim to fame is the artists who work on staff, ready to customize any existing pattern, or, for an additional fee, develop patterns tailored to individual tastes.

Secrets to Press Success

Every day, droves of press releases roll into newspaper offices. Most of them never see the light of print.

Why? A few reasons. They don't match the paper's news content. They run too long, with the nitty-gritty information buried somewhere on page 18. The writer forgot to include a contact telephone number, and the reporter finds himself with questions to ask and no one around to answer them.

You can dramatically increase the chances of your press release, or a version thereof, making it to print by following a few simple steps.

- Keep it short: As a rule, your press releases should run no longer than a single page.

- Follow newspaper style: Write up a paragraph or two answering the following questions: Who? What? When? Where? and Why? Make sure this paragraph appears at the top of your release. Here's an example: Smith Manufacturing announces the opening of its second location. The new factory, on 123 Maple Street, will open October 3rd. President Marc Smith said he needed a second factory because of the overall growth of his business....

- Address your press release to a specific person: A press release addressed to the Very Large City Gazette will likely be passed around and passed around until some reporter eventually throws it out. To avoid this, phone the newspaper ahead of time, and find out which reporter is in charge of sorting through business press releases. Address your information to that person.

- Include a contact telephone number: Remember, the reporter may have questions about your release. And, since reporters often work odd hours, you may want to list two phone numbers—one for day, one for evening.

Creative Wallcoverings advertises itself as the funky new decorating choice. It really plays up its on-staff artists. The company has also garnered some attention from local media outlets, and before you know it, everyone with a few extra bucks to spare wants custom wallpaper for her home.

You prospect for persons who've just bought a new home and for people who've lived at the same address for ten years or more, and who may want to redecorate. As you cold call, they recognize the name of your company, recognize its specialty. Those who like paint or plain white wallpaper will likely thank you for your time and hang up. Those who like the artiness of your wares will prove more receptive to your calls, and allow you to stop by for a presentation.

And Why It Doesn't Matter

Your product's position in the market may help get you in the door, but it won't, by itself, lead to a sale.

Because of advertising's very nature, you or your company has played up only a few pertinent features. If you wax poetic on all things wonderful about your product or service, you'll wind up with five-page newspaper ads and three-minute commercials. You waste an awful lot of money this way. And you end up boring the very prospects you hope to attract.

Once you've garnered an appointment, don't assume that you'll clinch the sale just because your ads have grabbed the prospect.

Your product has many features, some of them not expressed in your marketing campaigns. And your client has many needs, not all of them uncovered during your cold call.

You'll learn in chapter 7 how to ask strategic questions to uncover your prospect's hidden needs. For now, though, think of it this way:

The prospect may adore Creative Wallcoverings's funky designs. But he may also have three kids and need a "scrubbable" product. Or he may be planning a

huge party in a month's time and wants to make sure you can have **the house** papered by then.

Your company's marketing campaign does not address those concerns. **But you can.** In fact, you'll have to in order to close the sale. Uncover all your prospect's **needs,** then explain how your product or service fulfills them.

DIGGING for Gold: Targeting Your PROSPECTS

CHAPTER FOUR

Prospecting. You've heard the word. It conjures images of griz-zled '49ers panning for gold in Sutter's Mill, California.

Why the mass rush to Sutter's Mill? John Marshall discovered a large gold vein there. The area was a known—some might say *qualified*—source of the elusive metal.

Did some prospectors hunt for ore in, say, Omaha? Or Buffalo? Or Boston? Maybe. But they were dumb.

In the 1840s, 30 territories had already sought and received admission to the Union. The country had grown too big to hunt for gold willy-nilly. Smart prospectors traveled to areas they knew, or strongly suspected, would pay off.

Targeting sales prospects—or "sales prospecting"—isn't so different. You need to

develop a list of prospects that you know, or at least strongly suspect, will need your product or service.

Now, before anyone thinks "I got me a big ol' list right here," and pats his phone book, realize this: Telephone directories, as a rule, don't work.

Why not?

They provide only a list of the most unqualified leads imaginable. Sure, you've got the names and the numbers. But this is what phone books can't tell you:

- Who lives in working-class neighborhoods, and who lives in wealthy ones

- How long has the person lived there

- Whether it's a homeowner or an apartment renter

- What type of business Joe Blow, Inc. is

- Who works for Joe Blow, Inc.

- Whether Joe Blow, Inc. operates in a burgeoning industry, or a mature one

And the list goes on.

Think about it this way: Mary Cranston, proprietor of We Straighten 4 U maid services, probably doesn't want to waste time calling on households bringing in less than $25,000 per year. An overworked single mother making $23,000 as a secretary may well love the idea of hiring a maid, but she simply can't afford We Straighten's $15-per-hour rate.

To maximize your chances of success, you need to identify those people most likely to buy. That means finding prospects who have both the need and desire for your product or service, and the cash to pay for it. Relying on the phone book for your research is the equivalent of panning for gold in Manhattan. Did anyone ever strike a vein there? Who knows? But it sure isn't the way to bet.

Generating a qualified list of leads is a huge, time–consuming task. But the more time you spend generating that list, the better your sales–to–call ratios will flow.

Referrals are the best source of qualified leads. Far and away, hands down, no questions asked, the best source. But to get a referral, you need to have clinched at least one sale. And you will probably have to keep plugging away—devising your own list of leads—for quite a while before you reach the salesman's dream: a business based solely on referrals.

For now, let's pretend you've yet to make a sale. How do you go about compiling a list of leads?

Know Thyself, Thy Product, Thy Industry, and Thy Competition

Before you start finding the right prospects, you need to garner some general knowledge about your product, your industry, and your competition.

Product

You probably already know your product's features. "It's blue!" you think. "And we also make it in green, and purple, and orange!" "It's fast!" "It's got lotsa nifty little knobs on it!" "It's sturdy. Made to last!"

Nobody cares—least of all your prospect. He doesn't want to buy another widget. He wants to solve a problem currently plaguing his business. You need to stop thinking of your product as an amalgam of features, and start thinking of what customer needs it can fulfill.

Here's an example:

You represent Realreal Fast Modems, Inc. The company has just intro'd a new modem that operates on 200KB—allowing for connections far more speedy than those offered by any other unit on the market. The product retails for $1,500.

You call on Catherine Smith, the owner of a two-employee research-and-marketing

firm. Employees do most of their research on the Internet. You've shown off your product. Then,

> *You:* "So, as you can see, Catherine, these modems are really fast."
>
> *Catherine (salivating):* "God, I'd love to buy a few, but I just can't afford it right now. My employees are really overworked, and I'm going to have to hire a part-timer."
>
> *You:* "But it's really fast."
>
> *Catherine:* "But I can't afford it, what with having to hire a part-timer, and all."
>
> *You:* "But it's really fast."
>
> *Catherine:* "But I can't afford it...."

In this direction lies madness, a madness that comes from presenting your product as an amalgam of features rather than as a solution to a customer's problem. Try this approach instead:

> *Catherine (salivating):* "God, I'd love to buy a few, but I just can't afford it right now. My employees are really overworked, and I'm going to have to hire a part-timer."
>
> *You:* "Wow. How much is that likely to cost?"
>
> *Catherine:* "About twelve grand a year."
>
> *You:* "For how much work?"
>
> *Catherine:* "About fifteen hours a week."
>
> *You (taking out a pen and pencil):* "Let's figure this out, Catherine. Realreal Fast Modems operate three times as quickly as your current modems. So they'll save each of your employees two hours per day. That's a total time savings of four hours per day, or twenty hours each week. It looks like that would eliminate your need for a part-timer, wouldn't it?"

Catherine (looking over your figures): "Well…yeah. And you said these go for $1,500 each?"

You: "Yes. So by investing $3,000 on two of these modems, you'd actually be saving nine grand a year."

Catherine will buy. And you'll leave with the satisfaction that comes from solving a customer's problem—a satisfaction that would have been decidedly lacking had you simply peddled another product.

In addition to thinking about solutions, you need to consider certain "hidden" benefits of your product. These may not seem particularly important to you, but they could prove very important to a customer. They include:

- Warranties

- Quick delivery schedules

- Servicing

- Money-back guarantees

- Product support

- Anything else you can possibly think of

Competition

"Know thy enemy," the adage goes. Not to say that you look upon legitimate competition as "the enemy" but…it sure helps to know all you can about competing businesses, including their weaknesses. While you never, ever want to put down the competition (it makes a salesman sound small and bitter), knowledge of weak points can help you position your own products.

Frank's Business Machines, for example, cannot possibly compete with IBM on price. However, it can position itself as a more personal alternative—better service, better financing, and a personal relationship with the owner.

Industry

If you sell consumer electronics, you need to know that because of falling margins, the industry has turned a little "soft" lately. If you sell plywood to contractors, you'll want to know about housing starts in your territory.

Why take the time to garner this type of knowledge? These changes can affect your client's business, and you have to understand how your product can accommodate those changes.

If you sell prerecorded movie videos to retailers, you can learn whether the market continues to be hit-related, or if it has swung to the other end of the pendulum— with more people renting art films. You can inform your client of the latest trend and open up sales for yourself in the process.

Industry knowledge also helps you act as a reference person to your prospect or customer. (It never hurts to send him a clipping from a trade paper covering an issue that may affect his business.) It keeps you from looking stupid. Finally, industry familiarity serves as a jumping-off point for the "small take" section of your presentation. An opening line such as, "So, are you ready for Comdex?" (a computer trade show) can prove a more sincere opening line than your complimenting the prospect on her outfit, or the picture of her children.

The surest path to industry knowledge includes discussions with knowledgeable salespersons in your company and subscriptions to trade magazines. Don't know where to find the mags covering your industry? Check out Media Finder at http://www.mediafinder.com/mag_home.cfm

Here are some other sources of information:

- Product brochures

- Technical reports

- Internal reports

- Customer surveys

- Customer feedback

- Published articles

- Financial reports

Zeroing In—Targeting the Prospect

After you've completed some initial study on your product, your competition, and your industry, it's time to start zeroing in on the right prospects to target.

Again, you'll want to spend some serious time generating a list of qualified leads. Here are some places to start:

- *Reverse directories.* These telephone directories list phone numbers by street and area (unlike the blindness of a regular phone book). They prove helpful in targeting a given section of town. If you sell expensive items, you'll want to target wealthier developments. If you sell baby items, you'll concentrate on areas considered popular with young married couples. You may have a few of the directories lying around the office. If not, you can find them in the library and on several Internet sites.

- *Corporate World Wide Web pages.* These pages, posted as advertising tools by a number of private and public companies, can provide you with a ton of information.

- *City Hall/county government.* Put on your reporter's hat and get familiar with the plethora of records available for public view. Sell dishwashers to consumers? Check out local building permits to find out who's building a new home. Sell vacation/honeymoon packages? You might want to know who has filed for a marriage license. Questions about a prospect's reputation for paying vendors? Search lawsuits filed in local courts, or bankruptcy filings in bankruptcy courts. Want to learn about a prospect's personal worth? You can get a pretty good idea from the price he paid for his house. These documents are filed in your county property appraiser's

The Myth of the Murderous Cold Call

Ever hear the story about the murderous cold call? The one where the salesman rings up a prospect, but it just so happens that the prospect's wife has pitched some type of a fit. The poor husband has called 911, and the paramedics are on their way. Only problem, they can't find the house. At the exact moment that they're calling to get directions, the salesman phones, and the paramedics get a busy signal. Upshot of it is, the guy's wife died, choking on her tongue, while the salesman was trying to pitch a new pool table.

What, you've never heard this story before?

There's a reason for that.

It never happened.

The better your research, the more likely your prospect will welcome your cold call.

But you'll run into grouches along the way. You'll encounter people who yell at you. This is how you deal with the situation: Apologize for disturbing the prospect, say good-bye, and hang up.

At most, you will have caused the prospect a very momentary annoyance. You have not murdered anyone.

offices. And—this might sound unpalatable, but—you can learn more than you ever wanted to about a given prospect by wading through a divorce action.

- *Rosters: chambers of commerce.* COC rosters will provide you with the names of most business movers-and-shakers in any community. And by the way—you should join. This is called "claim staking." If you're the only architect in your local chamber, you'll get to know the personalities involved and, chances are, members will turn to you when it comes time to design their new homes. This takes time, but it works.

- *Rosters: clubs, fraternal organizations, social organizations, alumni groups, church groups, trade associations.* Sell pet supplies? Members of the local kennel club will prove a gold mine. Sell diapers? You might want to target the local Mothers of Twins club. This is obvious. What may not prove so obvious is actually finding these associations. Many of them are small, homegrown organizations that don't advertise, and don't even have a telephone number. To track them down, you may want to read "Club Meetings" schedules in your local newspapers. Also, many libraries maintain informal lists of the clubs operating in the area. Again, join and "claim stake" as many as possible.

- *Local business journals, business sections of local newspapers.* You know all those "Promoted" and "Welcome Aboard" columns that clutter up your local newspaper? Read 'em. Clip 'em. They can prove extremely valuable to the alert salesman. A bank gnome who has recently snagged a VP's post may well want to treat herself to a new car to accompany her new job, her new image. A corporate executive, a transplanted Arkansan who has just moved to your town, may be renting temporarily until he finds his dream house. There's no reason that you can't sell him his dream house. Or the furniture that goes in it. Or the sauna he wants to build in his backyard. For this type of research, the smaller the newspaper the better the chance it will carry the information you want. Also, depending on your industry, don't forget to check out the engagement/wedding pages, new births column, obituaries, and the like.

Cold-Calling Mentality

You've done your research. You call people who should have a legitimate interest in, or need for, your product.

And you get a grouch on the phone. A real grouch. She asks if you're a salesman. You say that, yes, you are a salesman—one who wants to fulfill her needs.

She tells you to go to hell, and hangs up.

What to do? A common way to deal with it is to sit by the phone for the next several hours, making absolutely no telephone calls, paralyzed by your fear.

It's a tried-and-true method. Problem is, you don't make a lot of money that way.

Rejection always hurts. Meanness always hurts. You need to get over it, and quickly.

Here are some common psychological techniques that can help:

• Hear the sound of cymbals banging.

• Hear an imaginary, quick swipe of fingernails against a chalkboard.

By associating unpleasant noises with rejection, you will less likely dwell on rejection.

You may also want to do something physical: Shake your head. Clap your hands once.

Put an end to your feelings of rejection, and get on with your work.

- *Library: Business reference sections.* Libraries stock a plethora of directories covering public and private corporations. These books include: Ward's Directories of Public and Private Companies, Dun & Bradstreet, Who's Who, The Encyclopedia of Associations, and many more.

- *Friends, relatives, acquaintances, business contacts.* Don't overlook the obvious. If your Great-Uncle Louie is itching to get on the Internet, and you happen to sell computers or Web TV—help him out!

- *Development organizations.* Also known as "Improvement Districts" and by other names, these quasi-governmental bodies operate in a number of cities and counties, helping to attract new business to the area. Call, stop by, and see what type of corporations will soon set up shop in your area. To track them down, call your local city hall.

- *Obvious users.* If your company has developed a new breed of piano, you want to hit all the music schools in town.

- *Trade shows.* Set up booths whenever possible.

- *"Dumped" customers.* Tom Hopkins, in *How to Master the Art of Selling,* describes this technique. Every business has turnover, your company included. What happened to the clients of sales personnel who've moved on? Chances are, many of them are probably sitting around, forgotten, in a file somewhere. Find the file, and re-initiate contact.

- *Smokestacking.* Visit local business and industrial parks to "sweep" them. See who has set up shop there, and determine if any of the companies have a likely use for your product or service. If you find any that look promising, stop in. No need to introduce yourself as a salesman at this point. Just say that you're looking for some information about the company. (Workers may well think you're a potential customer—and that's OK.) Pick up product brochures, corporate reports, and any other material readily available.

- *Mailing lists.* You can buy lists of likely clients. Check under "Mailing Houses" in the yellow pages of the (dare we say this?) local phone book.

Remember: Though mailing houses do some very good work, they are not nearly as concerned about your business as you are.

- *SEC Reports.* In the technological age, these reports are very easy to get. Just access http://www.sec.gov/index.html. What will you learn? Which public companies have done well this year and which companies are in trouble; which companies are expanding, and where; and the names of potential Yes Guys. The list runs on and on.

Other People Like You—Getting Referrals

The phone rings in your house. You pick it up. A voice on the other end says,

> "Hi. Mr. Jones?"
>
> *You:* "Yes?"
>
> *Sales Rep:* "Hi, sir, this is Susie Selkin calling from RevIt Motors. How are you today?"
>
> *You (hesitantly):* "Fine."
>
> You're not happy to speak with this person. You've already readied yourself for the pitch.
>
> Now look at this scenario:
>
> The phone rings. You pick it up.
>
> *You:* "Hello?"
>
> *Sales Rep:* "Hi, Mr. Jones?"
>
> *You:* "Yes?"
>
> *Sales Rep:* "Mr. Jones, this is Susie Selkin calling from RevIt Motors. Your sister, Becky, suggested I give you a buzz."
>
> *You:* "Oh, hi."

No matter how well developed your cold-call technique, no matter how much you've worked to target appropriate prospects, no matter how terrific your product or service, nothing gets you in the door like a referral. You may cite one of the prospect's

Corporate World Wide Web Pages as a Source of Knowledge

Today, many corporations—even tightly held private ones—post pages on the World Wide Web. Take retail chains as an example. Consumers access their Internet sites to find a directory of stores, find directions to the stores closest to them, look over offerings, apply for jobs, read the company's latest press releases, and sometimes even buy goods.

Companies post these pages as a public relations tool to attract consumers, not salespeople.

But salespeople will nevertheless find their own uses for these tools. You can use them to find the names of corporate honchos, leading you to the Yes Guy. You can review their offerings to see if your product or service would fill a niche. You may also read in a press release that Harry Smith Telemarketing, Inc. is opening a large, back-room office in your territory. Where you just happen to sell phone systems. Or desks. Or pens. Or any of the other items that Mr. Smith's 150 new employees will need.

How do you find these Web pages?

If you sell to very large, public or private companies, you might want to access Hoover's Online., at http://www.hoovers.com. This site links you directly to company Web pages. If you're targeting a smaller company, try to find it through any decent search engine. If you fail, try this technique: Plug in http://www.COMPANY NAME.com. You'll be surprised how often this works.

Finally, if you simply can't find a corporate Web page, call the company and ask if it has one. If it does, ask for the address.

friends or family members, one of her business associates, or even her boss. With a referral, you've found a way—a big way—to get the prospect's trust and attention.

In addition, sales referrals constitute qualified leads. Very few current customers will refer you to prospects who have absolutely no use for your product or service.

So, how do you get referrals?

You ask for them. At, or after, the close of sale, you ask for them.

This process is trickier than it sounds. If you simply ask a client whether he knows anyone else who needs a car/puppy/computer/lime-green business outfit, he will probably say "No," or "Not offhand."

Don't believe it.

Your customer probably crosses paths with dozens of people each week. But he will not, in the nanosecond it takes to respond to your question, review all those faces, all those personalities, or all those needs.

You, the salesman, have to help him narrow this throng of faces to a unit he can quickly access mentally.

Here's how:

> *You:* "Well, Harry, I'm sure you'll enjoy your new ski gear."
>
> *Harry:* "Thanks. I'm sure I will."
>
> *You:* "When are you gonna break it in?"
>
> *Harry:* "On Thursday. Five of us are taking a long weekend up in Killington."
>
> *You:* "That should be a blast."
>
> *Harry:* "You're telling me. They're predicting fresh powder."
>
> *You:* "Harry, let me ask you something. Do all your friends own their own skis?"

Harry: "No. Bobby's a newbie, so he rents."

You: "Do you think he'd be interested in buying anytime soon?"

Harry: "Yeah, I think so. He's new, but he's really getting into the sport."

You: "You mind if I take down his name? I'd like to give him a call. Maybe I can help."

Harry: "Sure. It's Bobby Harrington."

You: "Do you have his phone number?"

Harry: "Not off the top of my head, but he lives on Maple Street, here in town."

You (taking notes): "Got it. Thanks. Hey, what about your other friends? Are they happy with their ski equipment?"

Harry: "Most of them are, but Eleanor's really a pretty good skier, and she's using this old equipment."

You: "Why doesn't she trade up?"

Harry: "She keeps saying it's too expensive."

You: "Do you think she'd be interested in our financing plan?"

Harry: "You know, she might."

You: "Great. Can I get her name and number?"

Harry: "Muller. 555-5555."

You: "Harry, thanks an awful lot for your help. I really appreciate it."

Harry: "Welcome."

You: "Before I let you go, can I ask—are these people your regular ski buddies?"

Harry: "Well, them and my ski club...."

In this scenario, the ski-gear salesman has successfully narrowed down the hundreds of people that Harry knows to five who might have a real interest in his product. Then, with his last question, he hits a jackpot. A ski group operates in town. He'll get a name and number to call, and approach individual skiers as soon as he can—in

other words, immediately.

This scenario illustrates a direct-to-the-consumer sale, so the salesman concentrates on the consumer's personal interests and contacts. To-business sales run a bit differently:

You: "Margaret, thanks an awful lot. I'm sure this fax machine will work really well for your needs."

Margaret: "I'm sure it will."

You: "Just before I let you go, I wonder if you could help me with something."

Margaret (hesitating): "Uh, sure."

You: "This area of town is new to me, and I'm trying to increase my business here. I was wondering if you might know of anybody in this part looking for a fax machine?"

Margaret: "Um, sorry. Not off the top of my head."

You: "Have you heard of any new businesses moving in?"

Margaret: "Oh, yeah. There's a lot of tenant turnover here. In fact, one of my employees quit last month. Quit to start her own business. She's renting some space here, moving in on Monday."

You: "Do you think she might need a fax machine?"

Margaret: "She might."

You: "Do you mind if I take down her name and number?"

Margaret: "No, that's fine." (Thumbs through her Rolodex to get the information, gives it to you.)

You: "Thanks a lot, Margaret, that really helps. Do you know any other new tenants?"

Margaret: "Well...oh, wait. A new luncheonette is opening downstairs. I ran into the owner the other day. Nice lady; her name is Elizabeth."

Taking in Corporate Surroundings While "Sweeping"

You work for John Fawn, Inc. You sell derricks. You've "swept" an industrial park and, while "undercover," viewed two offices—those of Frank Mone Construction and Jerry D. Building.

The difference startled you. Walking into Frank Mone, you feel accosted by black lacquer and glass. Lithographs hang on the walls. The receptionist works behind a highly polished wood counter, manning an upscale computer and state-of-the-art telephone system. She is dressed professionally, in a well-tailored business suit. You tell her that you're looking for information about the company, and she hands you glossy, four-color brochures about both the housing developments and the custom homes built by the company.

Fifty feet and a world away sits Jerry D. You walk in. The receptionist, dressed in blue jeans, plaid shirt, and a baseball cap, sits behind an ancient, beat-up steel desk, pecking away on (and you may have never seen one of these before) a typewriter. He smiles as you walk in, and says "WhatcanIdoforya?" You tell him you'd like some information about the company, and he tells you, "Well, we did some real good work at the Hunting Woods development. Built 125 houses in six months, and boy, are those folks happy. Then we do some custom homes as well. If you're interested, I could give you some names and numbers." You take the names and numbers and walk away.

Clearly, you think, you have to target Frank Mone. Then you do a little research and learn that Frank Mone does about $30 million in construction each year, Jerry D., $45 million.

Every business conducts itself differently. Its overall style reflecting the tastes of its owner or corporate culture. You have to adjust your pitch accordingly.

You: "Maybe I'll stop by. I know a lot of restaurants allow you to fax in orders these days...."

Get Your Priorities Straight

With all the leads you've developed through referrals or research, you've realized you can't possibly find the time to personally call on them all.

That's OK. In fact, that's good. It shows you've done your homework.

Not all sales leads are created equal. You need to set priorities.

With hot prospects, you adopt a "Do Anything to Meet Them" attitude (examined extensively in chapter 5). But remember: Sales calls cost money (gas, mileage costs, tolls) and time—especially in travel and pre-call planning. Set priorities based on:

- Chances for success (based on your understanding of customer need/desire for your product)

- Geography

- Chances for sound referrals

- Itch cycles. "Itch cycles" are known buying cycles. These can be based on the life cycle of a given product or customer trends in replacement/buy up. Pretend you sell high-end stereo systems. You may know that the average consumer of these products will trade up his speakers every five years. After four-and-a-half years pass, start targeting that customer for repeat business.

Sometimes direct mail coupled with follow-up phone calls will have to do. This approach, used only with low-priority clients, works like this:

- Get the name of the Yes Guy (see chapter 5). Send him a personal note outlining what your product can do for his company. Attach product brochures.

Tell him when you plan to call.

Collecting Your Thoughts

If you work in an industry where you receive lots of incoming calls from prospects, the judicious use of the hold button can help you collect your thoughts.

Think of it this way.

You're a real estate agent and a new prospect, a businesswoman recently transferred to your city, has called to ask whether you list any three-bedroom homes on the east end of town. You know, off hand, that you list literally dozens of such offerings. But, instead of just saying, "Sure," and setting up an appointment, you may want to ask, "Can I ask you to hold for a minute, ma'am, while I check?"

Use a short hold time to quickly develop questions that will uncover your prospect's secondary needs, and narrow down your offering to match them. What else does your prospect want in a home? How many baths? How large a garage does she need? Would she appreciate a screened-in porch? A pool? Would she like to be able to walk her children to the nearest grammar school?

Think up these questions quickly, get back on the line, discover the prospect's un-expressed needs, and work to match your product to those needs.

Call him at the appointed time.

These procedures must be followed step by step. If you don't write a personal note, or don't include a call-back time, or don't follow through with the call-back, you're wasting your time, postage, and brochures.

Ice Calling

Striking fear in the hearts of (sales)people everywhere, cold calling nonetheless is a necessary sales tool.

But you hate it. Everybody hates it. You'll probably never grow to love it, but you can develop the mind-set and the skills that will make you comfortable with the process.

You may, personally, have had bad experiences on the "pick-up end" of cold calls.

"Hi," you hear on the phone. "This is Sweers, Ms. Smith. Since you're one of roughly six gazillion Sweers customers, you clearly understand the importance of life insurance. You need to protect your loved ones against the event of your untimely demise, Ms. Schmitt. Have you thought about that, Ms. Schmid? (No pause.) We have the option for you. As a valued Sweers customer, Ms. Smick, we invite you to join in this exciting opportunity. For only several hundred dollars a month, you can protect your loved ones, Ms. Schmicle. Isn't that important to you, Ms. Smeed?"

No, it's not. Not at all. You signed up for a Sweers credit card about a year back when you bought a stove, fridge, and washer-dryer combo. You don't want life insurance. Sweers has no reason to believe you want life insurance. In fact, you are a 32-year-old, single executive. No one depends on you monetarily. You have more than enough money in the bank to cover your burial should you, say, get hit by a truck on Tuesday. And these goofballs can't even get your last name right.

You never should have received this call.

The telephone book is the most unqualified list of leads available. The Sweers credit-card list comes second. Sure, it tells the salesman that you have reasonably good credit, but that's it. Hundreds of thousands of people get credit from this huge department store chain—all for different reasons. You wanted appliances. The next guy wanted to buy a girl a diamond—and make her his fiancée. Another woman just got her first big job and spent $500 on business suits. Finally, a 37-year-old biochemist needed credit to buy a stroller, playpen, and glut of baby clothes. He is the family's primary breadwinner.

This is the guy Sweers should have called, and undoubtedly did. The problem comes when the company dumps him, you, and all other card holders in the same category.

You wouldn't be that foolish.

When you cold call, take heart. You have developed a list of qualified leads, and before you even pick up the phone, you believe the people you have decided to call will actually benefit from your product or service. You will annoy some people. But you are far, far less likely to annoy people than Sweers is.

Let go of your fear, and believe you can help.

Cold-call scripts and techniques are discussed in the next chapter.

GETTING *an* APPOINTMENT

You represent FineHopps, a regional microbrewery, and boy, are you psyched for an upcoming presentation to Harry's Patio.

This New Orleans watering hole caters to an upscale clientele—a clientele that can fork over the $4 per mug your brews demand. And while the bar stocks a variety of imported beers, it lacks the dark lagers, a FineHopps specialty. You conquered your cold-calling fear, and managed to get an appointment with Tammy Taylor, the bar manager.

The presentation runs smoothly, because you've learned to listen more than you talk. You find out Harry's stock needs, and explain to Tammy how FineHopps can fill those needs. Tammy has slowly sipped your samples and found them to be superb.

Now, you go for the close.

You: "Tammy, just to sum up—you have a number of customers who like lager, and who'd like to be able to buy it here. You also mentioned an increasing demand for "home-grown" brews, and said you're looking to meet that demand to keep your customers happy. Finally, if I understood you correctly, you're always concerned about suppliers delivering beer when you need it. Does that about cover it, or have I left out anything?"

Tammy: "No. You're right on."

You: "OK, great. Now, as you mentioned, you think our beer would go over really well with the Harry's crowd. You said you'd order it yourself, on a night out. And I've also explained the personal attention our brewery gives each of its customers. If you have a particularly heavy demand one night, you'll have our beeper number. One of us is always on call, and we can deliver a couple of cases at three in the morning, if you need them. That would take care of your delivery concerns, wouldn't it?"

Tammy: "It sure would."

You: "Great! Tammy, it seems to me that Harry's Patio and FineHopps would make a really good match. Would you prefer we start delivery this weekend or next?"

Tammy (looking at you as if you'd just handed her a stuffed weasel): "I dunno. I don't make these types of decisions. Only Harry does. Our owner, I mean. Harry Harrison."

Your heart drops. You try to recover, but you're clumsy.

You: "OK, Fine. Let's set up an appointment for me to meet with Mr. Harrison."

Tammy: "Well, he travels around a lot. He owns thirty bars here in the South. He's only here about once every six weeks, for a day or two."

You: "Well, when is he expected in next?"

Tammy: "Two weeks."

You: "Can I make an appointment for that time?"

Tammy (shaking her head): "I don't think you have to do that. This is a

Finding the Yes Guy

Wife. Husband. Mother-in-Law. There's a Yes Guy in every family, and, if you specialize in direct-to-consumer sales, you need to find her.

Mary Masterson, real estate agent, has just become a buyer's broker for a young married couple in the market for their first home. The couple is into "urban pioneering." The area they have chosen may still seem a bit seedy, but they can feel movement, and believe that any home they purchase here will ultimately appreciate. Mary couldn't agree more. She does her research and finds five condos she feels appropriate for them.

Then she meets them, face to face, for the first time. Actually, she meets the three of them. There's the wife, the husband, and a very nice old lady: the 87-year-old grandmother who has generously offered to provide the couple's down payment for their first home. Mary recognizes the grandmother as the "Yes Guy."

She shows them the first condo on her list. This unit sits on the third floor of a renovated Victorian. It has three bedrooms, high ceilings, original moldings, and a built-in china cabinet. The price? $80K. The husband and wife practically turn cartwheels, they're so happy.

The grandmother, however, is winded and scowling, wrinking her nose in disdain at the area in general. Mary can practically read the grandmother's mind. She says to the grandmother, "Ma'am, you look a little concerned. Is there something you're unhappy with?"

"Well, yes," she says, and goes on to list her previously unspoken concerns. What can Mary say to alleviate this lady's fears? She can say what is true. "Ma'am, the building next door is now abandoned, but J-mart is taking it over in just three months." Or: "The purchase price includes a $1,500 assessment for an elevator and a doorman. The tenants' association has agreed that this amenity is needed here."

Mary Masterson has already sold the couple. Her brilliance lies in recognizing this family's Yes Guy, and addressing her concerns.

great product. I'll tell him all about it."

You: "I'd rather talk with him myself."

Tammy (a note of irritation creeping into her voice): "Well, I just told you I'd tell him all about it."

As you leave Harry's, you realize you have only two choices: You can either hang yourself, right there on Bourbon Street, or you can learn from your mistakes.

You made two mistakes.

• You Failed to Find the Yes Guy

A primary rule of sales: Only talk to the Yes Guy. You sold to the No Guy. Harry, the proprietor, may well respect Tammy's opinion. She's the one who draws the drafts night after night, while he travels around checking out business at all the bars he owns. Had your beer tasted like three-day-old dishwater poured into a mug, she could have told you, "No. We don't need it. We hate it. Leave us alone." She cannot, however, sign the contract and tell you to start deliveries Thursday. Only Harry can do that. You wasted your time talking to someone who can only say, "No."

• You Didn't Get the No Guy on Your Good Side

Once Tammy said she lacked the power to say yes, you took a confrontational attitude. You told her, "I'd rather meet with Mr. Harrison myself." Why didn't you just say, "Looks like I made a big mistake here, because apparently you're pretty much of a nobody"? That statement would have had the same effect on the bar manager.

You could have salvaged the sale after Tammy acknowledged she lacks the power to make purchasing decisions. It could have worked this way:

Tammy: "I dunno. I don't make these types of decisions. Only Harry does. Our owner, I mean. Harold Harrison."

You: "Oh sure, I understand. Is Mr. Harrison around, by any chance? Maybe we could go speak with him."

Tammy: "No, sorry. He's only around for a day or two every six weeks. He won't be in for another two weeks."

You: "Can we figure out a time when the three of us could meet then?"

Tammy: "Don't worry. I'll tell him all about it."

You: "I'm sure you will. And obviously, Mr. Harrison really respects your opinion—he made you his bar manager, after all. The only thing is, though, if I'm not in that meeting, then Mr. Harrison can't actually taste our beer."

Tammy: "Well…"

You: "Tammy, you'd like to order our product, wouldn't you?"

Tammy: "I really would, yeah."

You: "Then I'd like to ask you to meet with Mr. Harrison and me. As I said, he must respect your opinion and ability to have given you this position."

Tammy (pulling Harry's calendar from the wall): "All right."

In this scenario, you've made the No Guy your ally. You know she likes your beer. You've legitimately nodded to her authority in the company (if she couldn't handle a nightly throng of customers, or if she didn't know the difference between a piña colada and a Bloody Mary, Harry clearly never would have hired her). And you make her feel a part of your team by using the word "we" rather than "I."

Ways to manage people like Tammy—people who can influence, although not actually make, buying decisions—are examined in chapter 7.

First things first, though. Let's talk about finding the Yes Guy.

Getting to Yes (Guy)

Titles confuse as much as they reveal. What, exactly, is the job description of the "key grip" listed at the end of most movies? Or the British nobleman officially called "Silver Stick in Waiting to the Queen"?

DON'T STOP BY

As a rule, you don't want to just drop by the Yes Guy's office and hope he can spare a few minutes to hear your presentation. You're too busy to waste this type of time. Also, in-person "cold calls" may make you look unprofessional, or at least "un-hot." "How good can she be," the Yes Guy may think, "if she has hours to spend sitting around my reception area, twiddling her thumbs?"

Use the phone to set up a definite appointment. That's the rule.

Corporate titles prove a little more direct, but not much. A woman listed on SEC reports as the chief financial officer may seem like the Yes Guy to sales reps in the accounting industry. Unfortunately, her title doesn't also note that she passes off purchasing decisions to her second in command because she has neither the time nor inclination to meet with salesmen. Finding the Yes Guy can prove tricky. It is also necessary.

The easiest and least expensive tool for finding the Yes Guy sits right on your desk. It is the telephone. Let's assume that you've done your research, and swept some corporate parks. You've identified a business that has a legitimate need for your product or service. But you don't know the name of the Yes Guy, and don't plan to waste your time selling to the wrong person.

You pick up the phone and call the company.

In the next scenario, you represent a temp agency that places accountants with firms needing extra help during tax season. This is what you say:

Receptionist: "Good afternoon, Stimmins & Mike."

You: "Good afternoon. Do I have Stimmins & Mike's main office, or a satellite?"

You ask this question for two reasons. First, it is completely nonthreatening, and serves as a warm-up for the questions to come. Second, you know that most buying decisions are handled through corporate headquarters.

Receptionist: "You've got the main office."

You: "Great. My name is Ben Tandem, and I was hoping you might be able to help me."

As with other research methods, you are at this point under no obligation, moral or otherwise, to identify yourself as a salesperson.

Receptionist: "I'll try."

You: "Can you please tell me whether you ever hire accountants on a temporary basis?"

Receptionist: "All the time, especially around tax season."

You: "That's what I'm interested in—temporary employees. I was wondering, could you please tell me who's in charge of temporaries at Stimmins & Mike?"

Receptionist: "That would be Kirk James."

You: "Mr. Kirk James. And what's his title?"

Receptionist: "He's our director of human resources."

You: "Thanks. And can I ask who Mr. James reports to?"

Receptionist: "He reports directly to Ms. Stimmins, our senior partner."

You: "Thank you very much for your help today."

Note: You can also use this approach face-to-face, while sweeping.

Now you have two names at the company, either one of whom may act as the firm's Yes Guy. Who do you call first?

When in Doubt, Start at the Top

In the above scenario, can Mr. James really buy your service, or can he only recommend to Ms. Stimmins that the firm buy your service? You simply don't know.

When in doubt, you need to start as high in the organizational structure as possible. You need to start with Ms. Stimmins. You do this for two reasons. First, you know

Why the Purchasing Department Doesn't Work

Helen Taxter, a reporter with nine years' experience, has grown tired of beat coverage. Wanting to concentrate on magazine journalism, she puts together a package containing writing samples, a cover letter, and a resume. She plans to drop it off at *The New Englander*, the most respected news-opinion magazine in Boston.

She has to decide to whom she should deliver this package. She has a few choices. There's Martha White, head of *The New Englander*'s human resources department. Then there's Hamlin Brown, editor.

Helen wants the editor to look at her work. He's the one qualified to judge her research and writing skills.

Ms. White may be a superb head of human resources. But consider the variety of résumés that cross her desk every week. She sees applications from advertising salespeople, from delivery people, from graphic artists, from production supervisors, and, yes, from writers.

As a job applicant, you never want to put your résumé in the hands of human resources.

And as a salesman, you never want to put your proposal in the hands of a corporate purchasing department.

Think of it this way: Suppose you represent a company that has recently developed a revolutionary accounting software. Who do you think will have an inherent interest in your product—a corporate purchasing department, or the CFO's office?

You need to go the CFO, because the purchasing department won't have the expertise to decide whether your product is really worth the investment.

that, as the firm's senior partner, she definitely has buying power. But suppose she has given James the power to make all decisions regarding the hiring of firm personnel? No problem. She or her secretary will tell you that when you call. And then, when you phone Mr. James, you can honestly tell his "gatekeeper" that "Ms. Stimmins' office suggested I call."

Some salespeople, like some reporters, want to have a pretty good idea of what the answer to a question will be before they even pose the question. If you want to try to pinpoint the Yes Guy before making your phone calls, here are some places to start:

- Personal knowledge: If you take the time to claim stake Chambers of Commerce, community/church organizations and other clubs, you get to know the regulars. You get to know whether Harry Smithers, broker for Harry Smithers Real Estate, Inc., makes purchasing decisions himself, or whether he hands the job off to his partner.

- Industry knowledge: Do the Yes Guys in your industry tend to carry titles such as "Senior Executive in Charge of Purchasing," or are they simply called "President"?

- Corporate flow charts, business directories, SEC reports: Titles such as "buyer" can lead you directly to the Yes Guy.

Opening the Gate

Remember the age of nine-to-five workdays? That era is long past. People today labor longer than ever before. In order to actually get all that work done, they have to avoid interruption. So they erect barriers between themselves and the outside world.

These barriers—here called gatekeepers—often decide with whom an executive will meet.

Gatekeepers assume many forms, from receptionists to executive assistants, to voice-mail machines to security guards. You have to get the Yes Guy herself on the

phone to make an appointment. But to get to the Yes Guy, you have to get past the gatekeeper.

Here are some ways to do it.

Cite Previous Contacts with the Yes Guy

This is the surest way to get the Yes Guy on the phone. Here's how it works:

You work with Green Recycling, and you want to contract with Bob Johnson Industries, a manufacturer of ergonomic office furniture.

You call. His secretary answers.

> *Harriet:* "Hi. This is Harriet."
>
> *You:* "Hi, Harriet. This is Mark McGann with Green Recycling. Is Bob available, please?"
>
> *Harriet:* "May I ask what this is in reference to?"
>
> *You:* "Sure. I'm following up on a conversation Bob and I had at the last Chamber of Commerce meeting."

Citing a previous contact with the Yes Guy is a pretty powerful in. Harriet will likely transfer you to Bob. Let's talk for a moment, though, about an even more powerful statement. When you and Bob chatted at the last COC meeting, did he say, "Why don't you give me a call at the office? We can talk more about it then."? If so, you can tell the gatekeeper the following:

> *You:* "Hi, Harriet. This is Mark McGann with Green Recycling. Bob asked me to give him a call. Is he available please?"

This tactic also works with referrals.

Presell the Gatekeeper

If you have no prior relationship with the Yes Guy, you may have to presell his gatekeeper by describing your intentions in the broadest, least threatening terms possible.

Boards of Directors vs. Employees Who Actually Make the Decisions

"Only our board of directors can make purchasing decisions," you hear. You hear it more than once.

Don't believe it.

Boards of directors, boards of education, and county commissions usually don't make purchasing decisions. They usually rubber stamp purchasing decisions, based on the advice of employees and corporate executives whom they trust.

Anyone who has ever sat through an entire city council meeting is aware of this process. The mayor says, "Patty in personnel needs to buy 300 computer disks. All in favor say 'Aye.' Matt in maintenance needs 50 new mops. All in favor say 'Aye.' Alex in accounting wants 25 new adding machines. All in favor...."

And the list goes on and on.

Yes, the city council controls purchasing, but most run-of-the-mill buys don't even get discussed.

There are exceptions. You may hear heated discussions regarding major purchases, or purchases dealing with new technologies.

To sell to publicly held companies (governed by boards of directors) or to governmental agencies, you need to find the employee who acts as the de facto Yes Guy, and sell to him. If you are dealing with a major purchase, show up at the meeting where the governing body will make its decision, and present your goods all over again.

Clearly, when Harriet asks, "What is this in reference to?" you shouldn't respond, "I want to sell Bob a recycling program." This phrase will engender fear in the gatekeeper. She will think, "How do I know if Bob wants a recycling program? He might get annoyed with me if I interrupt him for a sales call."

Instead, frame your offering this way: "I want to talk to Bob about tax breaks his business can get from recycling programs." Now Harriet should feel comfortable putting you through to her boss. She'll be happy to help his company save money.

Make the Gatekeeper Your Cohort

You've cited your previous contacts with the Yes Guy, or you've presold the gatekeeper. She wants to put you through to her boss, but he's traveling. What to do? Make the gatekeeper your buddy. If she tells you, "Bob won't be in the office until next Tuesday," call back on Tuesday. Follow this script:

> *You:* "Hi, Harriet. It's me. Mark McGann from Green Recycling calling again. Is Bob in the office, please?"
>
> *Harriet:* "He is, but he's a little overwhelmed right now. He has a lot of work to catch up on. It's only his first day back."
>
> *You:* "Harriet, do me a favor. I'd really like to talk to him about the tax breaks that you and I discussed. When would be a good time for me to call?"
>
> *Harriet:* "Well, he usually works late on Wednesday evenings before his weekly squash game. You might want to try him between 6:00 and 8:00."
>
> *You:* "Harriet, I really appreciate your help."

Ask the Gatekeeper a Question He Can't Answer

Some gatekeepers know a good deal about the company they work for, and they are also very protective of their boss's time. In these cases, you have to be ready to ask questions the gatekeeper can't answer.

Look at this scenario:

Harriet: "Can I ask what this is in reference to?"

You: "I'd like to talk to Bob about some of the tax breaks available to businesses in this city that recycle."

Harriet: "Oh, no. He looked into that last year, and figured out that we'd lose more in recycling contracts than we'd get back in tax breaks."

You: "Oh, I see. Is he aware that just last month the City Council doubled the available tax break?"

Harriet: "I really don't know. You'd have to talk to Bob about that directly."

You: "I see. Is he available, please?"

Calling the Yes Guy When the Gatekeeper Is Out to Lunch

Sometimes no matter how friendly and positive your tone, no matter how compelling your product or service, the gatekeeper just won't put you through to her boss. But since executives often work longer hours than their gatekeepers do, you can wriggle around this problem by calling when the gatekeeper is unlikely to be at her desk. You may want to try calling early in the morning, after five in the evening, or during lunch. (Many executives will take lunch at their desks, while their secretaries eat out. It is hard for anyone to resist the lure of a ringing telephone. Chances are, the Yes Guy himself will pick up when his secretary can't.

Once You Have the Yes Guy on the Phone

A sound sales adage: To clinch a sale, meet face-to-face with the prospect. In general, you cannot make a sale over the phone. But if you sound unprofessional, if you sell too hard, or if you sound uninformed, you can lose a sale over the phone.

A rambling telephone discourse will also turn off your prospect. Your pitch should run no longer than one (count 'em, one) minute. If the prospect himself chooses to chat more, you accommodate him. But say what you need to say in a minute or less.

Here are the steps:

- Introduce yourself, greet the prospect. If you have an "in," this is the time to use it. "Mr. Johnson, this is Mark McGann with Green Recycling. I'm calling to follow up on the conversation we had at the last Chamber meeting." Or: "Mr. Johnson, this is Mark McGann calling from Green Recycling. Your colleague Greg Stevens suggested I give you a buzz."

- Uncover the prospect's needs. From your research, you may already have a pretty good idea of what these are. But asking questions confirms your research and allows you to have an actual conversation with a prospect, rather than your simply "selling at him." Here are some examples: "Ms. Newcomb, I understand your company hires temporary workers during peak seasons, isn't that right?" Or "Mr. Hyde, I understand your roof is about eight years old now. Is that true?"

- Wait for your customer's response. You may learn that your initial research was faulty. Ms. Newcomb may say, "We used to hire a ton of temporary employees, but the company has undergone a tremendous expansion recently. We've actually hired most of the temps. Now, we probably only take on six or ten temps a year." You will have to quickly adjust your sales pitch to fit your prospect's actual, rather than perceived, needs.

- Ask for permission to speak. Reply to your prospect's response with a phrase such as "I see." Or, when appropriate, "Terrific!" Then ask if they have a moment to speak with you. Promise to be brief. If the prospect says, "I have to get off the phone now," respond with, "I understand you're really busy right now. Would it be better if I called back at two o'clock or at four o'clock?"

- Give the pitch. Briefly outline your success stories within the industry. "We've been able to help several luncheonettes like yours, including Susie Eatz, attract a whole new batch of customers by stocking vegetarian sandwiches."

Dealing with Voice Mail

"You've reached the office of Ms. Karyn Tompkins. Please leave your name and number at the beep." BEEP!

How do you deal with voice mail?

There are two schools of thought.

The first says call back when you can speak to the prospect personally. "But," you say, "I call and I call, and I only ever get her answering machine." You may be calling at the same time each day, say 3:30 in the afternoon. Maybe your prospect has a regular meeting at that time. So call at various times throughout the day. "But," you say, "I do. I call every fifteen minutes from 8 until 6."

You have entered Voice Mail Hell. This is how you can escape the situation. Call the company's main number and say: "I've been trying to get through to your comptroller's office all week, and I only reach an answering machine. I need to speak with a real person in her office."

The receptionist will probably say, "Let me transfer you...." You'll respond: "Thanks, but before you transfer me, what's the number you're dialing? Just in case I get cut off." You'll be surprised how often this works.

Other salesmen, however, have found success leaving a series of recorded, scripted messages on answering machines. Their purpose is not to close the sale, but to arouse, in the prospect, enough curiosity that the prospect has no choice but to return the telephone call. Create a serial or a soap opera. Make your pitch in three distinct messages over three days, with the person on the other end hanging on for the punchline. If he discovers that he can't wait for your next message, he's even more likely to call you.

And always make it super-easy for the prospect to call you back—tell him exactly when you'll be in the office to receive his call.

- Respond to questions only in general terms. If you give the prospect all the information she needs over the telephone, she has no reason to meet with you. And if the prospect doesn't meet with you, you've all but lost your chance for a sale.

- Go for an appointment. Don't say, "When would you like to meet?" Say, "Would Wednesday or Monday be better for you?"

- If they absolutely refuse a meeting. Mail the prospect a personalized letter, detailing how your offerings have helped other companies in similar situations. Include a call-back time. Then call back. During the second phone call, again go for a face-to-face meeting.

How do these techniques pan out? In the following script, Mark McGann, the sales rep for Green Recycling, finally has Mr. Johnson on the phone:

> *You:* "Good afternoon, Mr. Johnson. This is Mark McGann calling from Green Recycling. I understand you're not currently taking advantage of any of the recycling programs operating in the city. Is that correct?"
>
> *Johnson:* "Sure is. Costs too much."
>
> *You:* "I understand. Do you have a minute?"
>
> *Johnson:* "Just one, and just barely. Things are really busy around here."
>
> *You:* "This will only take a moment. I'm calling, sir, because Green Recycling has been able to help a number of local businesses, including Harry Smith Industries, substantially reduce their waste-disposal costs. I'd like to stop by your office for about a half hour this week, to explain our program."
>
> *Johnson:* "No, I don't think so. I don't know what Harry Smith is doing, but we did some research on a recycling program about a year back, and it just wasn't cost-effective."
>
> *You:* "I understand that, sir. But have you read about Anytown City Council passing an ordinance doubling the tax breaks available for local businesses that choose to recycle?"

Johnson (surprised): "No, I haven't. I've been traveling all week. Doubled it, you said?"

You: "Yes. And with Harry Smith and many other industries in town, we've been able to work out programs that make our service pay for itself with reduced occupational taxes and lower waste disposal costs. Many of our clientele save money when they use our services. Everybody likes to save money, don't they?"

Johnson (chuckling): "Yeah. I'm not one to turn down money."

You: "Great. Mr. Johnson, which would be a better day for our meeting? Tuesday or Thursday?"

Johnson: "Don't bother coming over. Just tell me now how the program works."

You: "I understand that you're very busy, sir, but I want to put together the best possible program for Bob Johnson Industries, and I really can't do that unless I see your operation—see what your waste output is, and determine how much of that can be recycled."

Johnson: "I see your point, but Tuesday and Thursday are really hectic around here."

You: "Would Friday or Monday be better?"

Johnson: "Definitely not Monday. I like to hit the week running. I could probably give you a half-hour late Friday afternoon, when things slow down a bit."

You: "Terrific. How about four o'clock?"

Johnson: "That'll do."

You: "OK then, Mr. Johnson. I'll see you at four on Friday. Thanks a lot for your time today, and I really look forward to meeting you."

Johnson: "Likewise."

Or Do It by Mail

Some salespeople find a "cold letter" more efficient than a "cold call." In fact, these letters can prove very effective sales tools. Words written are generally more definitive and more memorable than words uttered.

Think of it this way: If you traveled to Madrid, you could probably still find a barfly or two who remembers, "In the early 1920s, there was this guy named Ernie sitting around. Lord, he used to tell the best stories."

That's great, and a nice anecdote. But if Ernie had only spun tall tales while sitting around a pub, he probably would have slipped from popular consciousness well before now. Instead, we remember his first name, Ernest, his last name, Hemingway, and his novels, from *The Sun Also Rises* on up.

As a salesperson, going for an appointment by mail can be effective. Your prospect gets a chance to read your ideas in black and white. And he may feel more receptive to an appointment once he has carefully perused, rather than just heard, your initial offering.

The first type of letter uses a "similar-situation scenario" to grab your prospect. It runs like this:

• The similar-situation scenario is an introductory paragraph outlining what you have done for a company facing similar issues as the recipient.

• The introduction is where you introduce yourself and your company.

• The reiteration is where you again note the salient points of your offering.

• Go for the appointment: Ask the recipient to meet with you.

• Close: Include a date when you will call to set up an appointment.

For these letters to succeed, you must follow each step as outlined above. Notably, present a similar-situation scenario before introducing yourself as a salesperson. A letter beginning: "My name is Joe Smith, and I'm a salesman with ABC, Inc." will likely head right to the circular file. Think of the similar-situation scenario as the "grabber," the paragraph that will make the recipient want to read on.

Here's an example:

December 4, 1999

Mr. Bob Johnson
President
Bob Johnson Industries
123 Maple Street
Anytown, Any State

Dear Mr. Johnson:

Harry Smith Industries' budget this year includes an extra $15,000 ear-marked for its crucial research-and-development department. This cash would have been wasted on trash-disposal costs. But Mr. Smith was able to salvage it from his garbage contracts by working with Green Recycling.

My name is Mark McGann, and I represent Green Recycling.

Here are some of the benefits obtained by Harry Smith Industries once it chose my company as a strategic business partner:

• Cash savings of $15,000

• Additional tax breaks offered by Anytown City Council to those businesses choosing to recycle

• Recognition as a "green" company by several regional environ-mental organizations

USE THE PHONE! LOSE SALES!

In general, you cannot clinch a major sale over the phone. You can't call up a successful executive, explain the merits of your yachts, and expect her to say, "Terrific! Deliver one to my marina on Tuesday!" Garnering a presentation appointment is the most you can hope for.

However, you can quite easily lose a sale over the phone. Your decision to talk too fast, sell "at the prospect," or indulge in a sales monologue will put the prospect off. He'll hang up the phone. And you've lost any hope of a commission.

Remember that the telephone is a powerful instrument. It can help you garner appointments, or it can cost you sales. To use it successfully, you must spend time honing your cold-call techniques.

I've researched Bob Johnson Industries and believe that Green Recycling can both help you cut your trash-disposal costs and open a new client base for you by boosting your image among area environmentalists. However, only by meeting with you in person can you and I decide for sure.

I'll call your office at 10 a.m. on December 14 to schedule an appointment. If you will not be available at that time, please leave word with your assistant, Harriet, as to when I may call back.

Thank you for your time, and I look forward to speaking with you.

Sincerely,
Marc McGann
555-1234

A second type of letter lets several key people in a business organization know that you are writing to each of them. It puts each on the spot a little, because if your product or service can truly benefit the organization, no one wants to be the one who drops the ball.

Here's the formula for a "leverage letter:"

- Send letters to several potential corporate "Yes Guys."

- Let each know you have written to the others.

- Briefly outline the salient points of

your offerings.

- Describe how you have helped other companies facing similar issues.

- Go for an appointment.

These letters run like this:

> December 4, 1999
>
> Mr. Bob Johnson
> President
> Bob Johnson Industries
> 123 Maple Street
> Anytown, Any State
>
> Dear Mr. Johnson:
>
> As a representative of Green Recycling, I am writing to you, your Executive Vice President, Greg Hoffman, and your Purchasing Department Head, Sheila Lopez, to see with whom I should meet for 25 minutes during the week of 14 December.
>
> Green Recycling offers its services to a number of large regional businesses, helping them:
>
> - Cut their waste-disposal costs
>
> - Take advantage of tax breaks offered by Anytown City Council to businesses who choose to recycle
>
> - Promote themselves as "green" companies, often garnering an additional client base in the process
>
> I've researched Bob Johnson Industries and believe Green Recycling can help you both reduce your waste disposal costs and enhance your image among area consumers with an environmental bent.

We currently do business with Harry Smith Industries, Long-Lite Manufacturing, and Industries Work, Inc. In each case, we have reduced their trash disposal costs by at least 18 percent.

If you agree to meet with me, you and I will together decide whether Green Recycling can bring the same savings to Johnson Industries. I will telephone your assistant on December 10th to set up the time. If you are not the appropriate person to speak with, please let your assistant know who is, and I will gladly contact her.

Sincerely,
Marc McGann
555-1234

Confirming the Appointment

Once you've actually gotten an appointment with the Yes Guy, you need to confirm it.

Don't bother the Yes Guy about this. Just place a quick call to his secretary to confirm.

And if you need some really obvious information, such as directions, don't even bother the secretary. Just call the business's main number and talk to the receptionist.

And How You Say It

Studies show that on the telephone, people listen more to the tone and timbre of your voice than to the words actually uttered. You need to examine your telephone voice and technique.

- Use the prospect's name. Use it early to grab the prospect's attention, but be careful about how often you repeat it. Ten thousand "Well, Mr.

Smith"s over the course of a 60-second call will sound like an obvious sales technique and leave a bad taste in the prospect's mouth.

- Moderate your tone of voice. In general, the deeper the better. But please, don't take this to the extreme. Don't sound like a heavy breather.

- Are you a loud talker? A soft talker? A too-fast talker? Keep a tape recorder on your desk to record your voice.

- Hear your smile. This may sound ridiculous, but a smile on your face reflects an attitude that your prospect can hear.

- Hear your (subtle) enthusiasm. Of course you feel enthusiastic about your product or service, and you should. However, embrace too much enthusiasm and you run the risk of "talking at" your prospect. Listen, talk, and turn the "cold call" into a real conversation.

FIRST
Impressions

CHAPTER SIX

In sales, this phrase is something of a misnomer. Ya got yer first first impression, yer second first impres- sion, yer third first impres- sion...and so on.

Don't assume your prospect forms his initial opinion of you, your product, or your company when you walk in the door.

He has already done his research.

He passively researched you when you made your cold call, listening to the tone and timbre of your voice, unconsciously analyzing whether you have a true interest in his business, or whether you simply plan to peddle another product. He has listened to the industry scuttlebutt about your company. This is your first first impression.

Your prospect may have also actively researched your company, for example, access- ing electronic newspaper databases to determine whether you're on the level. Maybe

he read your Web page to learn what your company does for other companies in his industry. This is his second first impression.

Finally, he sees you, in all your glory, walk into his office. This is his third, and most important, first impression. Your cold call may have seemed a bit clumsy, but cold-calling is an inherently awkward situation. The prospect can deal with that. Your press may not have been great—but who actually trusts reporters these days?

The force of your presence can overcome lukewarm first and second first impressions. However, a clumsy initial presentation will bring you down and cost you your sale, no matter how terrific your cold-calling technique and overall reputation are.

Think of it this way: You are Matthew Marc, CEO, salesman, and Jack-of-All-Trades for Marc Personnel Services, Inc. Your cold call was clear and succinct. Your press is sound because you saved money for the personnel departments of several area companies—all owned by family members and friends who look beyond your foibles to the service you provided.

This is your first presentation for someone who has no basic interest in you as a person.

You walk in the door. Your palms sweat. You wear a lime-green business suit. You are shy by nature, and are unable to look the prospect in the eye. You don't smile. You exude anxiety.

The tragedy is that you truly believe in your service, and you know that you can help the prospect. But he won't believe it. Your body language and overall personality imply (in this case wrongly) that you have nothing of worth to offer. And he will believe the impression, not the truth.

As discussed in chapter 1, sales is a craft like any other. You can learn to control your body language. You can alter your style of dress to suit professional standards.

And by working for a legitimate company, by selling a product you truly believe in, and by learning some simple public-relations techniques, you can largely control what your client may learn of you before you walk in the door.

First Things First

Passive Research

Here are some ways a client may subconsciously form impressions of you and your business:

- *Your telephone personality.* Remember, the tone and timbre of your voice, as well as the pace of your speech, make at least as much of an impression on your prospect as the words spoken.

- *Letters confirming your appointment.* Some salespeople telephone to confirm an appointment, others confirm through letters. If you choose the latter course your letter should have perfect spelling and grammar. The prospect's name should be spelled correctly in the salutation. Your letter should be freshly typed or printed out. (A photocopied form letter with the prospect's name hastily printed in looks exceedingly unprofessional.)

- *Brochures and newsletters.* You may have chosen to mail your prospect a product brochure or newsletter before your appointment, to "prep" him for the presentation to come. If so, make sure these materials suit your client's needs or desires. Say you sell boats. If your client has only an interest in and cash to pay for a small sailboat, you don't want to send him a glossy, four-color brochure detailing all things wonderful about your company's $95,000 yachts.

- *Your status in the business community.* Your client may have heard your name or your company's name before, whether through COC meetings, industry events, or social gatherings.

What does he hear at cocktail parties?

"The salespeople from Savvy Sportscars—God, they couldn't have been more helpful. It's not all that easy to find a maroon Porsche with a purple interior, but they were able to special order one for me. Sure, it took a little time, but I was real happy with the results. Then, about a year or so after I bought it, I started to hear this little

rumble under the hood. I took it in. You know what was wrong? A screw had come loose. The mechanic told me that. So he tightened it. He could have told me the belts were gone or the engine was going to fall out and charged me three grand. I wouldn't have known the difference."

Or:

"Savvy Sportscars? Oh, man, forget those people. I told them I wanted a maroon Porsche with a purple interior, and they didn't have one on the lot. They only had lots and lots of red Porsches with tan interiors. So they kept saying, 'No, no, you want the red one with the tan interior. It's really a better look.' So then I'm like, 'I'm the one who's going to drive this car for the next ten years. I know what I want.' The whole thing just left a bad taste in my mouth, and I ended up driving fifty miles to Motor Sports. They gave me what I wanted. If I were you, I'd do the same."

Remember, the best way to get a good reputation is to be reputable.

Active Research

Your client may actively research your company to learn more about your offerings and reputation. In most cases, you can play an active role in determining what he'll find.

- *World Wide Web sites.* If your company does not yet have a presence on the Internet, you may want to think about creating one. It lets clients know that your company keeps up with the times and serves as a great public relations tool. Besides listing your offerings and a few testimonials from some well-known clients, it should also offer regularly updated product and industry information. This could take the form of an article penned by your office scribe, up-to-date industry statistics, or anything else you can think of. Valuable, regularly changing information will keep prospects coming back to your site, and you'll garner some leads in the process.

- *Contacts with existing customers.* Did you note the name of a reference when cold-calling the prospect? Chances are pretty good that the prospect will actually call your reference after your initial telephone call. Similarly, if you did not actually cite a reference but pushed a hot button such as, "We've been able to help several businesses like yours, including May Flowers Florists...." expect your prospect will call May Flowers Florists.

A word of caution: You are a reputable salesperson. You do your best for every client, and then some. But, on occasion, mistakes will happen. Say a retailer ordered 75 yellow sundresses from your company. She opens the box, only to discover that you've gotten your orders confused, and have inadvertently shipped to her 175 purple sun dresses. You apologize, and rectify the situation ASAP. But this retailer is not a particularly forgiving person.

The upshot: Never, ever cite to a prospect or use as a reference the name of a client who is anything less than 110 percent happy with you, your product, or your service.

- *Newspaper and magazine articles written about your company.* Easier than ever in the electronic age, your client may decide to do a newspaper search to determine what kind of press your company has received. If you deal in commodities, he may do a general search of the product.

Here's an example: You represent a Joe's Ginseng, and you want to contract with J-Mart to stock this herbal dietary supplement on its endcaps. Joe's Ginseng, as a corporation, may have received little or no press, so your customer may research ginseng to learn about its reputation as an herb believed to increase energy and promote overall well-being.

You increase your chance of sales success by representing a company or a product with a proven track record.

Pre-Call Planning

Patty Wright's Music Studio has finally granted you a presentation appointment. The facility not only gives music lessons, but also stocks instruments. You represent Segovian, a mid-to-upscale line of classical guitars.

You've learned some presentation and closing techniques, and you feel they will serve you well in this meeting. And they will. But don't expect these techniques, and your charm, to carry you through. If you've not thoroughly researched the music-school industry in general, and Patty Wright's Music Studio in particular, these are some things you won't know:

- The National Endowment for the Arts has recently chosen Ms. Wright's advanced classes to play before the President of the United States during a Kids Rule festival.

- Ms. Wright's school has suffered declining enrollment.

- Whether parents are willing to spend more and more money for fine musical instruments for their children, or whether they have adopted a "start small" attitude—holding off on big-buck buys until the child proves his interest.

Consider pre-call planning a more intense version of the research work you did to develop a qualified list of sales leads. You can even use the same research means discussed in chapter 4. In general, you want to learn as much about your prospect's business and industry as possible. Industry changes often constitute new needs for your prospect's business, and you need to determine how your products can fulfill those needs.

Perhaps the most important aspect of pre-call planning is determining which of your products you will sell to the client.

Why bother to do this? Why not just present your entire product line and let the prospect make his own choice?

Easy. Your prospect wants to invest his money in the best product possible. Faced with a seemingly limitless array of goods, he will become confused. He will be unable to decide which product will best suit his business, and may simply decide not to buy at all.

You may have faced this phenomenon in your own life as a consumer:

Hail Fellow Poorly Met

"Hey, Jim," you say, clapping your prospect on the back. "How the hell are ya?" "Gorgeous family! Really terrific. That your wife? A beauty, a real beauty." Jim walks to his desk, presses a button on the intercom, and utters a single word. "Security."

No, probably not. Not even the worst first impression will have you dragged, kicking and screaming, out of a prospect's office. But the "slap on the back" first-contact sales approach is the very worst you can use. It reeks of insincerity. Complimenting a prospect on his children is an obvious gimmick—a way to get to the prospect's soft spot. Slapping a prospect on the back is a way to establish false intimacy, as is the use of Jim's diminutive nickname—Jimmy. Your motives here are as clear as glass—to establish false intimacy in the hopes of garnering a sale based on that intimacy.

Forget it. Think of your prospect as someone you want to help, but a newly met someone you want to help.

In every social interaction, people take small steps toward getting to know one another. Sales contacts are no different. When you arrive for your presentation, shake hands. Refer to the prospect as Mr. or Ms. at first, until you feel him or her begin to warm up to you. If you make any small talk at all, center it on business or industry issues of interest to you both.

This is not to say that your connection with a prospect won't warm up over time. If your prospect becomes a regular customer, and you meet with him once each month, you may begin to develop warm feelings for each other. That's fine. In fact, that's natural and good. You may discover a mutual love for baseball or fly fishing. Your families may interact at industry events. If that happens, then it's fine to spend a moment or two talking about the Mets, or asking how the wife and kids are.

You walk into a discount clothing chain, one that sells items remaindered from expensive department stores. There are great bargains to be found here—lovely clothes, from professional to casual—marked at a fraction of their original price. You've got some money in your pocket, and plan to treat yourself to a new business outfit. Walking into the store, you head over to the "business attire" section. You see no fewer than 25 racks of business wear. You paw through the first rack and find several garments you like. You paw through the second, and find several more, including a truly beautiful shirt that would nicely complement a pair of pants you failed to pick up from the first rack. You go back to the first rack to find them. Then you head to the third rack. You find several more items. By now, what was supposed to have been a pleasant treat for yourself is starting to become a chore. You are confused, tired, and thirsty. And you leave.

Think how this phenomenon could play out in your sales life:

You do your music school research and find out that the parents of classical-guitar students now tend to start their kids on mid-range instruments, holding back on a larger investment until students show dedication to the instrument. In your initial sweep of Ms. Wright's Music Studio, you noticed a hole in her inventory—she stocks lots of $150 classical guitars, and lots of $700-and-up classical guitars, but precious few mid-range instruments.

> *You:* "So, Ms. Wright, as you mentioned, more and more parents these days want to start their children off on mid-range classical guitars. They don't want really inexpensive models that will fall apart in two weeks, but they don't want to make a major investment until they're sure of their child's commitment to the instrument. Isn't that right?"
>
> *Ms. Wright (nodding):* "Yes. Yes, it is."
>
> *You:* "And you said that your music studio would like to stock more guitars in the $250 to $500 price range, didn't you?"
>
> *Ms. Wright:* "Yes. We're seeing more and more of a call for that range of instrument."
>
> *You:* "Great. Ms. Wright, Segovian will be able to help you. Let me tell you a little bit about our B-Major mid-range line. There are 24 instruments in that line. The B-Major 1 retails for $250, is constructed of pine,

and has a quite serviceable set of strings. The B-Major 2 retails for $275, is constructed of a slightly better grade of pine, has the same serviceable set of strings, and has a faux-pearl inlay along the neck. The B-Major 3 retails for $300, is constructed of yet another slightly better grade of pine, has a faux-pearl inlay and an upgraded set of strings. The B-Major 4 retails for $325, is constructed of yet another slightly better grade of pine, has a faux-pearl inlay, an upgraded set of strings, and raised markers on the frets. The B-Major 5…"

And on and on and on.

This salesman insists on telling his prospect about all the minutia inherent in every product in this line. How will Ms. Wright feel? Her eyes will start to glaze over. This bewildering array of choices will confuse her. She may decide not to decide. And you've lost a sale.

The presentation would run much more effectively if tried this way:

> *You:* "So, Ms. Wright, as you mentioned, more and more parents these days want to start their children off on mid-range classical guitars. They don't want really inexpensive models that will fall apart in two weeks, but they don't want to make a major investment until they're sure of their child's commitment to the instrument. Is that right?"
>
> *Ms. Wright (nodding):* "Yes. Yes, it is."
>
> *You:* "And you said that your music studio would like to stock more guitars in the $250 to $500 price range, didn't you?"
>
> *Ms. Wright:* "Yes. We're seeing more and more of a call for that range of instruments."
>
> *You:* "Great. Ms. Wright, Segovian will be able to help you. Let me tell you about our mid-range, B-Major line. It offers 24 products, but I think you'll be most interested in B-Majors 1 through 5. They run from $275 to $450. All of them offer a remarkably pure sound for that price range."
>
> *Ms. Wright:* "What accounts for the price difference?"

Dressing, and Driving, for Success

As a successful salesperson, you probably understand that your 1968 Beetle—you know the one you painted with neon-green smiley faces and day-glo pink-and-orange daisies—is probably best left for weekend excursions to the beach, and not for sales calls.

However, you may not realize that your 1998 silver Jaguar, gleaming in the sun, can also be inappropriate to the sales situation at hand.

It's too flashy. It says, "Look at how cool I am! Top of my game!"

Same with clothing. You'd never wear torn blue jeans and a halter-top or muscle shirt to meet with a client. Nor should you wear a gorgeous blue cashmere sweater with silver threads running through it. Again, the item is too showy.

When deciding what to drive, or what to wear, go for something that reflects a sense of quiet power. This means appointments that are classy, clean, and, in the case of dress, modest. They should enhance your image, but not take attention away from you, or your product or service.

When you meet with a prospect, you want him to think, "Wow, she's right. Contracting with PermaTemps really can help us figure out which prospective employees are right for this company." Not, "She spent more on that outfit than I make in a month."

You: "The quality of the pine. Also, there are a number of decorative features available in the more expensive models—faux-pearl inlays, that type of thing. We find that consumers are often willing to spend a little more for a guitar that not only sounds good, but also reflects their personal style."

At this point, you may think: "I'm not going to tell the customer what she wants. That's unethical. She will tell me what she wants, and I'll accommodate her wishes."

You're right. You're absolutely right. If a customer walks into your dealership saying that he wants a maroon Porsche with a purple interior—you want to do your best to get it for him. But all you know about Wright is that she needs mid-range guitars. In the above scenario, you've focused on that need and, based on your knowledge and experience, determined which items in your product line would best fill that need.

And Ms. Wright is not stupid. If you have presented to her products that don't actually match what she's looking for, your presentation will run this way:

You: "And you said earlier that your music studio would like to stock more guitars in the $250 to $500 price range, didn't you?"

Ms. Wright: "Sort of. We're seeing more and more of a call for mid-range instruments, but at the high end of the mid range. Say guitars that go for $350 to $500."

You: "I understand. Ms. Wright, Segovian will be able to help you. Let me tell you about our mid-range, B-Major line. It offers 24 products, but I think you'll be most interested in B-Majors 19 through 24. They run from $375 to $500. All of them offer a remarkably pure sound for that price range."

As a salesman, you do your best ahead of time to determine your clients' needs, and choose products most likely to fill those needs. However, sometimes the prospect will throw you a curve ball. Sometimes, what you perceive as her needs will differ from her actual needs. You have to be quick on your feet, conversant with your entire product line and services, and immediately tailor your proposal to what the client actually wants. Ways to address this dichotomy are discussed in chapter 7.

Once You Walk in the Door

"Stand up straight."

"Smile."

"Look people in the eye."

If these words sound like your Mom, there's a good reason. She was (and you know this by now) almost always right.

We've discussed different kinds of first impressions in this chapter. But the figure you cut as you walk into your prospect's office is far and away the most important first impression.

Bit by bit, here's how your first impression should flow.

- *Dress appropriately.* A three-piece Bill Blass suit may serve you well if you sell to legal firms. That same suit, however, may seem off-putting if you sell to high-school football teams. Try to tailor your dress to suit your prospect's industry. Sometimes an upscale look may be appropriate. In other industries, it would be better to adopt today's "professionally casual" style.

- *Relax.* You've already made inroads. If your prospect didn't think you were worth his time, you wouldn't have been invited to meet with him. He wants you here. You are welcome.

- *Stand up straight.* You could sell the definitive cure for cancer, but if you hunch your shoulders or lower your head the prospect will believe you have no confidence in your product.

- *Smile.* A man tends to clench his jaw when he gets annoyed. Unfortunately, he breaks his jaw in a car wreck. The doctors have to rewire it. He walks around for six weeks, constantly annoyed. Why? His jaw is constantly clenched. Flip this story around 180 degrees. You smile when you feel confident. Even if you don't feel especially confident, forcing yourself to smile will lift your spirits, preparing you for your presentation.

- *Look the prospect in the eye.* We've all heard the phrase "shifty-eyed sales-man." Turning your glance away from your prospect may indicate you're being less than honest with him. Some of us, because of upbringing or personality type, feel uncomfortable looking someone in the eye, no mat-ter how reputable we may be. This is a skill, and, like any skill, it can be learned. Practice on your friends, your spouse, your children, and your co-workers.

- *Shake hands.* A firm handshake, so they say, indicates sincerity. And that's true. However, do not take this to the extreme. Your handshake should be warm and caring. It should not be a bone-crunching contest.

- *Hand prospect your business card.* It never hurts to have your name and phone number in front of him.

- *Don't sit down until your prospect does.* This is a sign of respect on your part.

- *Business-based small talk.* Depending on a prospect's personality and over-all demeanor, some salesmen like to spend a moment chatting before beginning their presentations. There is merit to this: it often puts a prospect at ease. If you choose to use small talk at the beginning of your presentation, it is best to talk about something professional. Don't say, "So, are you betting on the Dolphins or the Giants?" (You don't even know whether your prospect is a football fan.) Instead, find something of common professional interest. If you are selling to a buyer at the Home Trolley home improvement chain, you might want to ask, "So, are you ready for the Home Builders' Show?"

How do you know whether your prospect is amenable to this type of chat?

Understanding body language and personality types is addressed in chapter 7. For now, though: If your prospect responds to your question about the Home Builders

Show with several words or phrases such as "Not yet. It's really hard to determine which buyers' time will be best spent there," it's probably OK to chat for a moment or two further. If he replies to your initial question with the word "Yes," you know he doesn't want to indulge in this type of small talk, and it's best to get right down to your presentation.

ASKING Questions

CHAPTER SEVEN

Here's an old chestnut: Four people gather at a cocktail party. One talks. What do the other three do? Wait to talk.

"Listening" differs from waiting to talk. And as a sales pro, you need to truly listen to your prospect in order to uncover his needs. In any successful presentation, you listen far more than you speak. But you can't just enter an office and say, "Ms. Nelson, I am now completely at your disposal. I am a very willing ear. So chat away."

Her silence will deafen you. Such an offer presents her with an unimaginable array of possibilities. What should she talk about? The secretary who quit Thursday because her boyfriend got transferred to Montana? The C- her eldest son received on his latest math test? The old friend who has given up the corporate world, traveling to Tibet to meditate with the monks? Or the fact that, while her current office manager does a quite competent bookkeeping job, he is absolutely unable to put together a tax return

that includes all the legitimate breaks available to Nelson's business?

As a representative of Accountants R Us, which of Nelson's life issues most interest you?

The process of listening is inexorably tied with the process of asking questions. Frankly, you don't care whether Nelson's son flunks math. You are not a tutor, and therefore you can't help her with that concern. You can, however, satisfy her accounting needs.

You need to lead your prospect into discussions of issues of concern to her that you can legitimately help with. You do this through strategic questioning.

Questions advance your sale in four ways:

1. They keep your prospect involved in your presentation. It is much more difficult for a prospect to "tune out" if he is called upon to respond to the queries you pose.

2. They help your prospect determine for himself the value of your product or service.

3. They indicate your sincere interest in the prospect's business.

4. They help you uncover your prospect's needs.

Be sure not to indulge in a sales monologue, or you'll risk selling goods a prospect doesn't really want. Use of strategic questions all but eliminates this pitfall.

Consider this scenario:

You represent Cumfy Cushions, Inc., a regional manufacturer of sofas. You've secured an appointment with Rhonda's, a small, start-up furniture store in your area. The business is so new that it has not even opened its showroom yet. Therefore, you've found little information about this operation from standard research means.

Here's your monologue:

You: "Rhonda, thanks so much for taking the time to speak with me today. I really appreciate it."

Rhonda: "You're welcome."

You: "Let me take a moment to tell you about Cumfy Cushions' latest line, Laid Back. As I'm sure you realize, the overall trend toward furniture design today is this: People want bright colors in their houses. They're tired of the muted same-old, same-old. We're helping to fulfill the desires of today's consumers with our Laid Back line. Any color your customer may want—we got it. Deep reds. Purples. Yellows. Bright, bright pinks. And here's the real kicker—we provide our retail partners with a customization program. If your customer wants the couch with the pink base—terrific. If he wants all-pink cushions—no problem. But, through our program, you can allow him to design his own sofa. If he wants the pink base with pink seat cushions and purple back cushions, no problem. If he wants the pink base with alternating pink, purple, and yellow cushions, no problem. We customize each sofa for no additional cost. We'll have it in your showroom two days after it's ordered. And talk about price! Our standard sofa goes for only $350. Isn't that terrific?"

Rhonda: "Umm, well...."

You: "Is there something I've not explained completely?"

Rhonda: "No. It's just that, well...I'm sure your product is terrific for younger people. But as you know, there are many retirement complexes around here. I plan to specialize in selling to a more mature clientele— people who live on a fixed income. I'm trying to stock the classics they like at a reasonable price."

You: "Oh."

You may as well shake Rhonda's hand and leave now. Even though Cumfy Cushions does in fact have a line of classic furniture, you've already all but blown your chances with this prospect by so strongly touting the Laid Back line. Any discussion about Cumfy Classics will now seem an afterthought.

Imagine how much more smoothly your presentation would have proceeded had

Tie 'Em Down

When you were a little kid, you liked recess more than any other class period, didn't you? Sunny spring days often make you happy, don't they? By now, you're probably beginning to wonder why I'm talking like this, aren't you?

The above phrases are tie downs—statements with a question tagged onto the end to engender a response from the prospect. Because it's much harder to tune someone out when you are regularly being asked to respond to their questions.

Use tie downs to keep your prospect involved. But don't use them so often that they begin to sound like an obvious psychological technique. That would turn your prospect off, wouldn't it?

Another tie-down warning: Only use them when you know what your client's answer will be. Suppose you sell health insurance to corporations. You are in the middle of a presentation to a small-business owner. You say, "As a conscientious employer, you probably want a top-of-the-line health plan for your workers, don't you?" But he responds, "No. There's no way I have that kind of money. Do you know what it's like being a small-business owner these days?" Don't fall into this type of trap.

Tie downs can fall at the end of a sentence ("Everybody needs water, don't they?"), at the beginning ("Wouldn't you agree that we all want a fair wage for our work?"), or even in the middle ("The earth, wouldn't you say, is round?"). Here are some standard tie downs:

Isn't (he, she, it)?

Don't (you, they)?

Wouldn't (you, he, she) say?

Wouldn't (you, he, she) agree?

you adopted a question-and-answer strategy:

You: "Rhonda, thank you so much for taking the time to speak with me today."

Rhonda: "You're welcome."

You: "I wanted to take a moment to talk about your business, if that's all right. You told me during our telephone conversation the other day that you wanted to stock sturdy, relatively inexpensive furniture. I don't know, though, exactly what styles of furniture you're looking for, or what type of clientele Rhonda's plans to serve. Could you please tell me a little bit about your plans for your business?"

Rhonda (nodding her head): "Sure. As you probably know, there are lots of up-and-comers living around here. But I think that most of them head out toward the chains, you know, Rooms-a-Go-Go, that type of place. But there are also tons of people living in those retirement communities out on Route 111. My mother lives in one of those, herself. She wanted to buy new furniture about a year back, but the offerings at places like Rooms-a-Go-Go seemed a little too flashy for her taste. And she lives on a fixed income, so the boutique furniture stores are way out of her price range. It was a real hassle finding the type of furniture she likes at a price she can afford. That was no surprise—she told me all her friends have the same problem. I did some research and found out she was right. That's when I decided to open Rhonda's. I'm going to serve that type of clientele."

You: "I see. And you think that sturdy furniture is important to more mature customers?"

Rhonda: "Yeah. You and I might buy a $300 couch, figuring we'll keep it for a year or two, then trade up. My clientele comes from a generation that wants things to last. I mean, my grandmother kept her living room furniture for thirty years, under plastic sheeting. I know this is a tall order, to find something that's sturdy but inexpensive, but I also know that there are manufacturers out there who can help me."

You: "There sure are. I want to ask you one more question. What do

you mean by inexpensive? What do you think your customers would be willing to pay for a couch?"

Rhonda (laughing): "I guess that word is a little vague. It doesn't have to be cheap, but I won't be stocking too many Louis XIV love seats, either. I think that my customers would be willing to spend in the $450 to $600 range, as long as they're convinced the product will last."

You: "Great. Rhonda, Cumfy Cushions will be able to help you. I want to spend a minute talking to you about two things: first, our Cumfy Classics line, which, I think, offers the overall look and usability that your clients are asking for, in the price range you discussed. I also want to chat for a second about our Perma-Clean process, which makes the furniture stain-resistant. Is that OK?"

Rhonda (leaning forward): "Sure!"

Types and Times

You don't ask a prospect, at the end of your presentation, "Will you please tell me about your business, your clientele, and your plans for the next five years?" It would hardly prove worth the breath. Similarly, you don't want to open your presentation by asking, "Would you prefer delivery on Tuesday or Thursday?"

Questions come in different types—broad, focus, value, multiple choice, porcupine, and obligating—and you need to employ them at different points in your presentation.

The Broad View

Employ broad questions early in your presentation to gather some general knowledge about the prospect and his operations. If preliminary research has yielded little information, these questions may be very broad. If you've unearthed a ton of information, you may adopt a more narrow focus in your opening volley.

Suppose you sell cell phones and have secured an appointment with a new medical practice, TLC. The practice is so new that all you know about it is its existence. Your first question may run something like this:

> *You:* "Dr. Thomason, thank you for taking the time to meet with me today. I'd like to pick your brain for a minute. Can you please tell me the exact nature of TLC's practice?"
>
> *Dr. Thomason:* "Well, Dr. Lawrence, Dr. Carrol, and I are all pediatricians. We've worked as junior partners for years, but recently took the plunge and opened our own practice. We find that new parents these days want a personal relationship with their childrens' physicians, and we want to offer those types of relationships."
>
> *You:* "I see. And how does this relate to your communication needs?"
>
> *Dr. Thomason:* "Parents don't want to call us and reach an answering service. They want to call us and reach…well, us."

If you know a little more about your prospect, you may embrace a more narrow focus:

> *You:* "Dr. Thomason, thank you for taking the time to meet with me today. During our telephone conversation, you mentioned that communication issues are of the utmost importance to your practice. Would you explain why that is?"
>
> *Dr. Thomason:* "Well, there are only three doctors in this practice, and one of us is always on call. But we all have lives. None of us plan to sit by our phone every night, just in case a patient might call to say that his child has the flu. We need cell phones that cover a pretty broad range."
>
> *You:* "I understand. What type of a radius are you looking for?"
>
> *Dr. Thomason:* "Our current carrier provides 50-mile coverage, which in theory is OK. Not great, but OK. But it doesn't always work. Last weekend, when I was on call, I was having dinner with my husband about 35 miles from my office. My cell phone never rang. Later, I learned that a patient's mom had tried to call me. Turns out that within that 50-mile radius there are blind spots, places where calls just can't be put through."

If you have uncovered a plethora of written information about your prospect, or if your cold call proved particularly fruitful, your broadest questions can seem pretty specific.

> *You:* "Dr. Thomason, thank you so much for taking the time to speak with me today. You mentioned during our telephone conversation that all the physicians in your practice carry their own cell phones, but you're dissatisfied with your current service. Would you please tell me the cause of your dissatisfaction?"

> *Dr. Thomason:* "Sure. Our cell phones only cover a 50-mile radius. That's just not enough. It's not uncommon for any one of us to visit with friends who live 60 miles from the practice. On top of that, even if you work hard to stay within the 50-mile radius, there are coverage "blind spots." Our current carrier can't provide a better service, so we're looking for a new one. My partners and I sat down the other day and decided we needed cell phones that covered a 100-mile radius, with no blind spots."

Narrow It Down

You've uncovered, through your use of broad questions, Dr. Thomason's communication desires—a cell-phone service that provides uninterrupted coverage within a 100-mile radius of her practice. Any number of units in your line provide that type of coverage. At your presentation's mid-point, you need to focus on your client's secondary needs to decide which products you will present to her.

These focus questions are used like this:

> *You:* "Dr. Thomason, from what you've just said, I understand that your primary communications concern is uninterrupted coverage within a 100-mile radius, is that correct?"

> *Dr. Thomason:* "Yes. Yes, it is."

> *You:* "Before we proceed, could you please tell me what other cell features might be important to you?"

> *Dr. Thomason:* "What do you mean?"

You: "Let's look at it this way. Suppose, one day when you're on call, you inadvertently leave the cell phone at the office. Or the battery goes dead. Would you prefer that your patients reach your voice mail, or that they be immediately transferred to one of your partners?"

Dr. Thomason: "I'd want the patient to be transferred to another physician. Definitely."

You: "And suppose a patient is trying to get through to you while you're chatting with a friend. Would you rather the patient be transferred to another physician, or would you prefer a call-waiting system that lets you handle up to three telephone calls at once?"

Dr. Thomason: "Call waiting."

The salesman in the above scenario first correctly employed broad questions to determine his prospect's overall needs, then focus questions to determine secondary concerns that the prospect, on his own, might not have considered.

Everyone Has His Value

Toward the end of your presentation, you want to get an idea of what type of value a prospect places on a product or service. This loosely, but only loosely, translates into what the prospect is willing to pay for it.

Don't, at this point, bring money into the equation. If you ask a prospect, "How much would you be willing to pay for this product?" he will respond with, "Not much," or, "As little as possible," or, "That new roof? Looks like it should go for about 100 bucks."

With few exceptions, people don't like to shell out money. Humans want goods, but they tend to balk, at least initially, about paying for them.

Prospect don't believe salesmen who insist on touting the value of the products or services proffered. Conversely, those prospects will believe it themselves once they have determined the value of the salesman's wares.

Don't push the value of your product on your prospect. Instead, lead him to discover its value for himself.

Consider the diamond industry as your model in this area. A diamond is nothing but a piece of pressed carbon. However, no diamond salesman markets his wares that way. He won't tell a budding Romeo, "Don't you think this piece of pressed carbon is worth five grand, you know, because of its rarity, and the expense of the treatment process, that type of thing?"

Of course not. No one would ever buy one.

Instead, knowing that diamonds in our society act both as status symbols and, rightly or wrongly, a sign of a fiancé's love for his betrothed, the diamond industry again and again runs advertising campaigns along the lines of, "Show her how much you love her." This type of slogan leads the consumer to determine, for himself, the value of a diamond. He loves his fiancée a lot, and will pay to make her happy—pay, in many cases, through the nose.

However you feel about diamonds, engagements, noses, or carbon, you can't deny the success of these campaigns.

In chapter 8, "The Presentation," you'll find information on how to get your prospect to actually pay for your wares. For now, though, consider how you can lead your prospect to determine the value of your product or service.

> *You:* "Dr. Thomason, I need to ask—lots and lots of practices use voice mail and answering services. Why is it so important to you that your patients have immediate access to the physician on call?"
>
> *Dr. Thomason:* "Well, you know, we're a start-up business like any other, and we need to differentiate ourselves from the pack. There are a lot of pediatricians here in town, and most of them practice very fine medicine. As do we. But we needed something other than the quality of our medicine to set us apart. We decided to market ourselves as the most caring practice out there. That means if a mother is hysterical because her first-born child is suffering from colic, she can get us on the phone, right away."

A, or B, or C?

Used later in your presentation, these questions entail your presenting your prospect with choices from your product or service line.

From the potentially broad array of services or products offered, you should present only the two or three that you believe best fill your prospect's needs. More choices than this may confuse your prospect, and he may decide to not decide—i.e. to not invest. For a full discussion of this phenomenon, see chapter 6—First Impressions.

The salesman in the Dr. Thomason scenario has already learned that the physician wants uninterrupted coverage, along with ring-back and call-waiting features. Here, he determines which products will most likely suit her interests.

> *You:* "Dr. Thomason, I understand, from what you've said, that personal contact with your patients is the practice's utmost concern. Isn't that right?"
>
> *Dr. Thomason:* "Yes. Yes, it is."
>
> *You:* "We offer a variety of cell phones and cellular services, but I think you'll be most interested in Cell Contact 101 and Cell Contact 102. They both provide uninterrupted service within a 100-mile radius, and both offer call waiting. The difference is in the ring-back feature. Should you be unable to answer your phone, the Cell 101 will forward calls to one other party. The Cell 102 will transfer calls to two other parties, each in turn. Which would you prefer?"

At this point, you may wonder why you bother to use a multiple choice scenario. Why don't you simply explain the merits of the Cell 102, the option you're sure Dr. Thomason will prefer, and ask if you can deliver on Tuesday?

Easy. When you offer only one option, you in effect ask your prospect whether he wants your service—yes or no. He will virtually always reply in the negative.

Porcupines

Don't assume that you'll be the only one asking questions during your presentation. Your prospect will pose a few of his own.

Consider any query posed to you as an opportunity to more deeply uncover your prospect's needs. Therefore, you should never directly answer a question until you've learned your prospect's reason for asking it.

Here are some examples:

> *Prospect:* "Do these dresses come in a full range of pastels, or only the peach and pink you've shown to me?"
>
> *You:* "Is a full-line of pastel shades important to you?"

Or:

> *Prospect:* "So, do all cars of this model have power windows?"
>
> *You:* "Do you want a car with power windows?"

Why bother to throw every question back to the prospect? While you know the rationale behind every question you ask, you do not know the rationale behind your prospect's queries. He may not be probing to make sure that you offer features he likes. He may be trying to determine whether your company plans to foist upon him features he doesn't like, want, or need.

Your client has handed you a porcupine, a prickly, unknown creature, and you want to hand it right back.

If you wax poetic to your prospect about the number of sundress colors available, or the joy of power windows, they may simply respond: "Oh."

But this is what they may think:

"So many manufacturers ask me to buy representative garments from their whole line. These other colors are nice, but peach is the hot color this year. I really only want to stock those."

Begging for "No"

In general, you never want to ask a question a prospect can answer with a "Yes" or a "No." Why? He'll choose no. Virtually every time, he'll choose no.

This is a psychological phenomenon. If you offer to someone the choice of spending money or not spending money, he'll choose to not spend money. That's why you need to offer a client multiple choices. Given a choice between yes or no, he'll pick no, and you've lost a sale. Given a choice between product A or product B, he will pick either A or B, and you've won a sale.

Look at this scenario:

You sell television sets retail. A client walks in and falls in love with your big-screens. He's always wanted one, he says, to watch Metropolitan Opera productions up close and personal. And now, for the first time in a long time, he's flush. You stand between two models and explain the relative merits of each. You think he's leaning toward the Big Screen Alpha. You pat it proprietarily and ask, "So, sir, would you like to take this home with you?"

"Uh, no," he says. "I'm not sure. I have to look around. Thanks though, thanks a lot."

If instead you had asked, "So, sir, would you prefer the Big-Screen Alpha or the Big-Screen Beta?" He probably would have chosen either Alpha or Beta, and you will have either closed, or at the very least advanced your sale.

This principle plays itself out through the entire sales process.

While cold calling to set up an appointment, you don't ask "Can I come by Thursday?" The prospect will say no. Instead you say, "I'd like to stop by. Will Tuesday or Thursday be better for you?" He will likely pick Tuesday or Thursday.

Or:

"Power windows completely freak me out. Suppose the car goes into the water? The electricity will short, and I won't be able to get out."

Answering a question before you uncover a prospect's reason for posing it may also drive you into an unnecessary frenzy of worry when your product doesn't have the attribute discussed.

Let's return to the Thomason scenario.

> *Dr. Thomason:* "Let me ask, do you folks offer caller I.D. on your telephones?"

"Oh God, we don't," you think. "And she asked about it, so she must want it. How do I handle this? Should I explain to her that a caller I.D. feature will be on line in six months? Suggest to her that she just hang on, because we're offering the service she most desires—a 100-mile, blind-spot-free call zone?"

Don't give yourself a migraine. If you return Dr. Thomason's question with the question "Is caller I.D. important to you?" she may well reply with the following:

"No. Not at all. I think you only need that type of feature if you're being stalked. But I know that a lot of cell phone companies include it in their overall packages, and really, I don't want to have to pay for a service I don't like."

Let's switch the situation around 180 degrees. As a salesman, you must recognize that on occasion a prospect may ask for a secondary feature that you just don't offer. Here's how you handle that type of situation: You tell the truth. But how you relate that truth to your prospect centers on the sale's overall scheme.

Here are some examples:

> *Prospect:* "Do these dresses come in a full range of pastels, or only the peach and pink you've shown me?"
>
> *You:* "Is a full line of pastel shades important to you?"

Prospect: "I like to offer my customers as broad a range of choices as possible."

You: "I understand that. And I need to tell you that we only manufacture these dresses in pink and peach. We've limited the colors because our marketing department has researched this season's tastes, and has found these are the hottest colors among the young clientele we cater to. We think it's better to provide our retail partners with colors we know will sell well, rather than with a bunch of different colors that will just sit on the rack."

Or:

Dr. Thomason: "Do your cell phones offer a caller I.D. feature?"

You: "How important is that to you?"

Dr. Thomason: "It seems like a nice feature, depending on how much it costs."

You: "Dr. Thomason, you've told me that your most important concern is uninterrupted coverage within a 100-mile radius. We can absolutely provide that, along with the call-forwarding and call-waiting features we discussed. Unfortunately, we don't, at this moment, offer caller I.D. on cell phones. However, plans for that feature are in the works. We should have it on line in six months."

Dr. Thomason: "That'd be fine. As I said, it's a nice feature, but it's not that huge a deal."

Obligations, Yours and Theirs

You're closing in on a prospect. He operates a chain of nurseries. He asks if you can deliver 2,000 yellow rosebushes to his distribution center by a week from Tuesday.

Don't, despite the call of your adrenaline, say "yes."

Instead, you need to ask the following: "If I can promise to deliver 2,000 yellow rosebushes to your distribution center by a week from Tuesday, will you agree to hire Ronald's Roses as your primary supplier?"

This is called the obligating question—perhaps the single most important moment in any sales call.

Obligating questions follow an if-then pattern. They constitute your making a promise if the prospect agrees to advancing the sale. He can advance to the actual purchase, or to another step in the buying process. You should determine what your goal is in asking the obligating question.

An obligating question is an essential step in closing the sale. Some prospects will ask questions all day long, then follow them with an infinite list of objections. You could spend weeks answering them all, especially if your prospect enjoys posing questions and objections solely for the sake of posing them. Then, after you've answered every conceivable query, you'll begin a long dialogue on price.

Frankly, you don't have this kind of time.

You certainly want to allot a reasonable amount of time to each client. But some people dither, and chat, and question, and dither some more.

You have to regain control of the sales process. You have to either advance, or uncover the prospect's true concerns. Obligating questions can prove a valuable tool.

Use an obligating question to begin winding down interactions and head toward a sale.

If, after three or four objections, the prospect says, "Well, I'm not sure it'll work for our industry," say, "Sir, if I can show you to your satisfaction that many others in your industry are using and enjoying this product, are you prepared to move ahead with an investment today?"

The prospect may respond, "Yes." If so, you're golden.

If he says, "No," you can ask, "I see. Sir, what other concerns do you have?"

This gives the prospect a chance to list his true objections—objections you can overcome.

You also must obligate the prospect to some type of advancement before you perform any significant work on his behalf.

Here are some examples:

You sell computer systems to governments and large corporations. Your hope to outfit City Hall's human resources department, and are speaking with its director, Peter McManus. You near the end of your presentation and he says:

> *Peter:* "I think your system is terrific, and I completely understand how it will free up a lot of my subordinates' time. I've been looking for something like this, because we're at a point where I really need my assistants' help in interviewing job applicants. But you know that all purchases have to go through the City Council. With smaller purchases, they're happy to just rubber stamp most of my decisions. But we're talking about $20,000 here. Council members are going to want to have some type of report in their hands—explaining how your computers have helped other personnel departments—that type of thing."
>
> *You:* "If I promise to put together that type of marketing study, will you promise to recommend that the City Council invest in this computer system?"

Or:

You represent Joey's Lumber Yard. You want to act as primary supplier to Western Builders, a company that constructs custom-built houses. You meet with George Nicholai, owner.

> *George:* "Look, you've told me a little about Joey's and I know your reputation is really sound. I like what you have to offer, and frankly, I'm looking for a new supplier. Our current supplier just blew us off, and if I don't have 850 two-by-fours at the construction site in three hours, I'm really off schedule. Right now, I'm calling in every chit I have."
>
> *You:* "George, I'm sorry to hear about that. But let me ask you something. If I can get those two-by-fours to your site by 4 p.m. this afternoon, will you agree to contract with Joey's as your primary lumber supplier?"

You may be thinking right about now, "I don't need to secure a commitment before I do this work. I'll just draw up the marketing study, or deliver the lumber. My prospect will be impressed by my professionalism. That will be enough."

That's a bad way to think.

You need to secure a commitment because your prospect is asking you to perform a considerable amount of work. You want an assurance that you will see a pay-off for your efforts.

If you had simply acquiesced to McManus's request to develop a market study without securing a promise from him, how do you know that, while you're busy researching and scribbling, he won't be interviewing other computer suppliers?

Without his promise to recommend your product to the City Council, you might wind up making a phone call like this:

> *You:* "Hi, Peter. This is Crystal Davis calling from Work Eaze computer systems. I just wanted to let you know that I'll have that marketing study on your desk on Thursday."
>
> *Peter:* "Oh, Crystal. Sorry. I meant to call you. I decided to go with ABC computers. Thanks a lot for your time, though."

Without having secured a promise from George at Western Builders, you might have overworked your colleagues to distraction, giving them only three hours to saw up 800 two-by-fours. Then you arrive at the construction site.

> *You:* "Well, George, it took some doing, but here are your two-by-fours."
>
> *Frank:* "Hey, great! Thanks an awful lot. What do I owe you again?"
>
> *You:* "Well, $920, but when we sign the paperwork, we can spread that out over time."
>
> *Frank:* "Look, I can't commit to that yet. I need to get some other quotes, meet with some other companies. So let me just write you a check for the $920."

Secure a promise to advance or buy before you perform a significant amount of work on a prospect's behalf.

Finally, the obligating question is vital when dealing with price. For example, if someone says, "Can I get a discount on this? Like maybe 10 percent off?" you may feel tempted to start negotiating on price before your prospect has even agreed to buy.

Big mistake. Instead, ask, "If I can get my boss to agree to a 10-percent discount, are you prepared to buy this today?"

In addition, be sure to repeat all the objectives you have heard the client express then end the question by saying, "And if our product can meet all those objectives, are you prepared to move ahead today?" This ensures that you truly understand the salient issues and puts your client on the spot: Is he really buying or just looking?

It takes some courage to ask obligating questions, but the payoff, in both sales and advancements, is well worth it.

How It Pans Out

So far, we've discussed the six basic types of questions employed during sales presentations: broad, focus, value, multiple choice, porcupine, and obligating.

Questioning is an important part of the sales process. However, don't think you only need to use questions properly in order to clinch a sale. You also have to deal with a few little issues such as "Answering Objections" and "Closing Techniques." These are addressed in the following chapters.

For now, though, you need to see how these questions pan out. Let's pretend you've met the Prospect from God: She's crazy about your product, poses no objections, and simply begs to write you a check.

Note: This never, ever happens in real life.

Notice in the following scenario how the prospect fails to give you all the information you need after your first broad question, so you pose another. Often this will

happen in actual sales presentations. Don't expect that you only have to ask one of each of the six questions described previously. The number of any single question-type posed will vary from presentation to presentation.

In the following situation, you represent A Smile A Day calendar company, a manufacturer of unusual organizers sold to independent gift shops. You're presenting your wares to Jan Tipkin, proprietor of the Queen of Hearts Gift Shop. You've greeted each other, and sit down.

> *You:* "Jan, I was wondering if you would please take a moment or two to tell me a little bit more about your clientele. You mentioned on the telephone that you serve mostly women, and that they come from high-income households. Tell me a little bit more about them. How old are they? What are their interests? Which of your product categories sell best?"

> *Jan:* "I'd say that most of my clients are in their early 30s or older, and by and large, they're stay-at-home moms. A lot of them do volunteer work when the kids are in school, but overall, their kids, their husbands, their friends, and their homes are their lives."

> *You (nodding):* "I understand. Would you please tell me what they're looking for when they come into Queen of Hearts?"

> *Jan:* "Cards first. These ladies really enjoy communicating with their families and friends, making them feel special. They send cards for everything. All the birthdays, weddings, and special events. But just to say hi, too. In fact, a few years ago we started selling a line of cards called 'Just for Everyday,' and they sell like hotcakes."

> *You:* "I see. So cards are your most popular product category. But you said on the telephone that you were hoping to beef up your selection of organizers. Why do you see that need?"

> *Jan:* "Because a lot of my clients run their homes and their families the way you and I might organize a business. Their kids go from school to piano lessons to swimming lessons. And on and on. The moms are trying to organize all this—plus their own lives and interests, and their husbands' lives and interests…it can be a nightmare."

You: "It sure can. But let me ask: You already have a nice selection of organizers and calendars here. Why do you need more? Do you find that your current selection isn't filling your customers' needs?"

Jan: "You know, they're really not. First off, they're all very sleek. They only come in black, brown, or blue. My customers are looking for something a little brighter, a little more decorative. They want more of a household accessory than a business accessory. Second, these organizers are geared toward corporate, rather than household, concerns. My customers don't need sections to record mileage, or stuff like that. The last thing is, they're all just meant for one person. They're meant for you to buy when you only need to organize yourself. My clients are trying to organize the lives of four, five, or six people."

You: "And that's a big job, isn't that right?"

Jan: "Huge."

You: "All right, Jan. So far you've told me that your clients are looking for organizers meant for several people, and that they'd like a more original, casual look than currently available on a lot of daybooks used in the corporate world. Is that about right?"

Jan: "Exactly."

You: "OK, Jan, so fill me in just a little more, if you would. Besides the features we already mentioned, are there any other features your clients would like in their organizers?"

Jan: "Well, a lot of my clients who have several children are always telling me how difficult it is to keep track of birth certificates, immunization records, that type of thing. And when kids are small, you always need to keep accessing that type of information. Being able to record it in an organizer would be nice."

You: "Jan, A Smile A Day will be able to help. I'd like to talk to you about our Home Page line of organizers. There are 15 products in that line—basically, hard-back organizer covers, all with three-ring binders inside. The decorations on the outer covers represent everything from English country gardens to Chagall paintings. The covers retail for about $9 each.

The inside is empty, each specific section sold separately. Of course, we'll provide you with a full sampling to sell here at the store. These sections cover everything from master calendars, to calendars for individual family members, to household accounts. The other section options just go on and on—and include places to record immunization records, birthdays, report cards, and so on. That sounds as if it would probably meet your clients' needs, doesn't it?"

Jan: "Sure would. Let me ask you, when I contract with your company, will I carry all 15 binders?"

You: "Would you like to carry them all?"

Jan: "Yes. At least at first. But eventually I may only want to carry 5 or 10 different binders, depending on what sells and what doesn't."

You: "That's easily manageable. Every month, we'll contact each other. When it's time to re-stock, you simply tell us how many of each binder you'd like."

Jan: "That sounds perfect. I'm more concerned, though, about the different sections. I don't know if I have room to carry them all."

You: "That's not a problem, either. We provide a book that you can keep on display, listing each of the 125 sections offered. Your customers can order any sections you choose not to stock."

Jan: "That sounds great. Unfortunately, though, my space here is very limited. How do I know which sections to stock?"

You: "From what you told me, and from what I see here, I suggest our multi-section packs. I think you'd most like either our Grow-Up Family pack, which covers the organizational needs of families with children up through age 16, or our Grown-Up Family pack, which covers families with children ages 17 and up. Which would you prefer?"

Jan: "I think the Grow-Up Family packs. Most of my clients have children of that age."

You: "Great! Is there anything else I've left out, anything you'd like to talk about?"

Jan: "One thing. Mother's Day is coming up in just three weeks. That's the only time men come into the store, they're always looking for gifts for their wives. I think these would sell terrifically, but I'd need to have them in stock at least two weeks ahead of time. Could you have 200 binders and the section packs here within a week?"

You: "If I can get you those binders and section packs within a week, would you agree to keep a full rack of binders in your store for a year?"

Jan: "Absolutely!"

THE *Presentation*

CHAPTER EIGHT

Unless you live in a major city with an excellent public transportation system, you probably own your own car. And if you're married, two probably sit in your garage.

Married couples will take on the additional expense of a second car, racking up a total of eight doors to feed, two banks to pay, and two insurance bills each month because they feel they need two cars.

Susie will say, "Sammy starts work at 8:30 in the morning on one side of town, and I start at 8:15 on the other. Then afterward he has his workouts at the gym, and I have my errands and my yoga classes. Sure, it would be great to drop one car and pocket the savings, but we really need both."

No, they don't. They could get by on one car. They could leave the house at 7:30 each morning, Susie dropping Sammy off at his place of business, then driving across town to hers. In the afternoons, Sammy could catch a ride to the gym with his work-

out buddy. Sure, he only puts in about 45 minutes each evening, and Susie's errands and yoga class take a total of two hours, but he could hang out and wait. Sit by the pool, read his newspaper, maybe do some prep work for the next morning.

Susie and Sammy don't need a second car. They *want* one. They have determined that the convenience, the ability to sleep an extra few minutes each workday morning, and the weekend freedom two cars provide is worth the cash they outlay.

This freedom has, for them, a value of at least $600 each month in second car costs.

People truly need very little.

If you run a two-person office, you could, conceivably, get by on two pens. If you're very careful not to misplace them, they might last for weeks. When they run dry, you buzz over to the office-supply store to buy another pair.

You only need two pens. But you want to have a whole box to chew on and lose as you see fit.

Or say you're an entrepreneur, currently working 11 hours a day at an enterprise that has truly taken off. You hire a part-time secretary to answer phones, type, and file for four hours each workday. You spend $9,000 a year for this service. You say you need it. But you don't. You could answer your own phone and up your work hours to 15. But, relishing the little free time you now have, you just don't want to.

So far we've talked about filling customers' needs. Now realize this: want is also a need. That's why people buy Porsches and furs and diamonds. What needs are you filling if you deal in luxury wares? A prospect's need for status, to look good, to keep warm in style. These desires are true needs for them.

Why do people buy anything?

From corporate executives to secretaries, people only buy if they have a want or a need that is important enough to justify the expense of the purchase.

The purpose of your presentation is twofold: to uncover your prospect's needs, and to demonstrate how your product meets or exceeds his desires.

The trick is getting him to pay for your wares. You can make high cost more palatable by directing your conversation away from price and toward value. Few people like to "pay for" anything. They will, however, willingly "invest" in a product or service once their needs are understood and the product is linked to them.

Convince your prospect of the value of your wares. Your customer is not interested in an amalgam of features. That's where cost comes in. "OK. So this car has a leather dash. How much extra do I have to shell out for that?" He does care about achieving his goal—that's a value issue. Remember, his goal could be anything from saving time to performing his job more efficiently to owning a Mercedes that will turn his neighbors green with envy.

Let's say you sell photocopiers. You have received an invitation to present your wares to Joe Blow Industries, Inc., a regional manufacturer of very important widgets. Everybody uses his widgets, so Joe Blow's business is booming.

How you present your product will be determined by how Mr. Blow expresses his needs, revealing his value hot buttons.

Here are some examples:

> *Joe:* "My secretary is spending too much time at the copier. It only spits out about 15 pages a minute. It's practically an antique. So while she's in the photocopying room, I'm left to answer my phone. This old clunker is wasting both of our time."

> *You:* "I understand how that can be a challenge, Joe. And let me tell you that the TrueCopy 6 will fix it. It spews out 100 copies a minute. And if you need to photocopy, say, a hundred-page report, you can just stick it in the feeder and walk away. Each page will be photocopied automatically. No need to stand there and copy page one, copy page two, and so on."

Or:

> *Joe:* "You know, I spend about $1,000 a year maintaining this antique. I just can't afford it anymore. I've got to get my office expenses in line."

You: "Yes. That's a big concern for a number of my clients. Joe, because we can offer you a payment plan on the TrueCopy 6, and because it comes with a three-year unconditional warranty, I think you'll find that investing with us will actually save you money."

Or:

Joe: "I just don't get it, but, for whatever reason, more and more of my prospects are demanding full-color presentations and marketing studies. I mean, we've always taken pride in the information presented, but everybody seems to be as concerned about the look of our study as the information."

You: "I know. As the world gets more sophisticated, it seems that everyone wants everything full-color and glossy. The TrueCopy 6 will be able to help you with that. It produces very clear four-color copies for a very reasonable investment."

Don't look at your presentation as an opportunity to show off your wares. Instead, uncover your prospect's needs or desires, determine what his goals are, and help him meet his goals.

Every sales presentation follows a general formula. First, you greet your prospect and make any small talk you think appropriate. Then:

- Define the focus of your conversation. Your prospect has allotted you a portion of his time for a reason. Something in your early marketing, or cold calling has piqued his interest. You need to manage the conversation so it focuses on that interest, not veering too far into incidental territory. Therefore, define the parameters of your conversation early on.

- Ask strategic questions. After defining the boundaries of your conversation, use the strategic questions discussed in chapter 7 to discover your prospect's needs.

- Link your product to the prospect's needs. This is easier than it sounds. Your prospect needs a photocopier. You sell photocopiers. Don't assume that you've done all the matching you need. You also need to tailor your pitch to fit your prospect's mind-set. You want to help him reach his goals. What does he want in a photocopier? Speed? That means he wants to save time. Color? He may want a more professional look for his business presentations.

- Hit value hot buttons. Position your product to fit your customer's mind-set.

- Use brochures, charts, and other types of visual aids. Remember, these are only support materials. Handouts don't sell, you do! Be careful when you distribute this material to your prospect. When it comes time for you to speak, you want his attention focused on your words. But if you hand him a brochure as you begin your speech, he'll read it and ignore you. Better to hand him a brochure as you near the close of your presentation. Use it as a tool to get to the same side of the desk as your prospect. Literally. As you near the end of your presentation, take out your brochure. Instead of handing it across the desk to your client, stand up, walk around to his side of the desk, put it between the two of you, and use it to "clarify" something you said. Something like:

"Harry, we've discussed the range of colors these outfits come in. Let me show you how they look so you get a true feel for the range."

Standing or sitting, on the same side of the desk as your prospect has a strong psychological effect on him. You're no longer salesman and prospect—you're a team.

- Answer objections. Learn how to respond to "We can't afford it," "I need to get other quotes," and similar quibbles by perceiving them as requests for more information. Common objections and ways to overcome them are discussed later in this chapter.

- Direct discussions away from cost, and toward value. Nobody likes to spend. This word connotes money wasted. People like to invest—they expect a return for a cash outlay. They want to see a value return on their checks. Remember: "value" means different things to different

EVERY "NO" MAKES YOU MONEY: SALES AS A NUMBERS GAME

Sales is a numbers game. You know that. Early on in your career, you should start tracking certain sales ratios: Number of cold calls to appointments garnered, number of presentations to closings, number of hours worked to money earned.

For the sake of discussion, let's say that your cold-call-to-presentation ratio and your presentation-to-close ratio each run one to ten.

This is how you can learn to love people who hang up on you, or who end your presentation with a firm, "I don't want it."

The nine who say no are stepping stones to the one who buys.

Without the nine who say no, you can't get to the one who says yes.

Every no makes you money.

prospects. To a law firm partner, it may mean client satisfaction. To a gentleman sailor, it may mean the prestige of a new yacht. You need to focus your value discussions to suit your customer's mind-set.

- Close or advance the sale. Each presentation should end with some type of advancement. You may advance to an on-the-spot close, or you may advance to another step in the buying process. Closing techniques are addressed in the following chapter.

Focus

You must direct your conversation with your prospect. You cannot allow him to wander for long into tangential subject matter. Otherwise, he may ramble on about his kids, his wife, and his golf game. Before you know it, he's showing you the door—and you haven't even had the chance to present your wares.

Define the scope of your conversation by stating, straight out, why you're meeting with the prospect and what you hope to accomplish during the meeting.

It works like this:

You: "Martin, thank you very much for taking the time to speak with me today. You mentioned during our telephone conversation that your business is looking for a reliable courier service, one that can guarantee getting your packages across town within two hours of a phone call to our office. Could we talk about that for a moment?"

Martin: "Sure."

You: "Can you please tell me a little bit about your business, and why a reliable courier service is so important to you?"

Notice how, in the above scenario, the salesman flawlessly makes the transition from defining the scope of the conversation to asking his first strategic question—a broad query meant to elicit information about Martin's business.

If your prospect granted you an appointment because you hit a hot button during your cold call—such as a direct referral or your success story with a similar business—now is the time to reiterate it.

You: "Martin, thank you very much for taking the time to speak with me today. You mentioned during our telephone conversation that your business is looking for a reliable courier-service program, similar to the one we've developed for your colleagues at Louis & Wright. Can we talk about that for a moment?"

Ask Questions

Throughout your presentation, you need to ask strategic questions in order to uncover your prospect's needs, to determine which of your wares best fulfill those needs, and to link the two. Question-and-answer strategies also help keep your prospect involved in your presentation. You'll employ at least five types of questions: broad, focus, value, multiple choice, porcupine, and obligating, along with tiedowns. These questions, along with the appropriate time to employ each type, are thoroughly discussed in chapter 7.

Link the Product to Your Prospect's Needs

You call on a prospect who says she needs a fax machine. You sell fax machines. You think you've earned your commission even before you walk in the door.

Hold up.

You need to link your product to your customer's needs, even if her expressed needs seem to meld perfectly with your wares. Lead her, through the use of strategic questions, to understand exactly what she's looking for in a product, then explain how your product matches her desires.

In the following scenario, you're meeting with Rachel Means, proprietor of Means Business Consultants.

> *You:* "Rachel, thank you very much for taking the time to speak with me today. You mentioned during our telephone conversation that your business needs a fax machine. Can we talk about that for a minute, please?"
>
> *Rachel:* "Sure."
>
> *You:* "Exactly what are you looking for in a fax machine?"
>
> *Rachel:* "The ability to fax people stuff."
>
> *You:* "I understand. I'm sorry, my question should have been more specific. I meant to ask, why do you want to fax your clients rather than sending them documents through e-mail or regular mail?"
>
> *Rachel:* "Well, first off—when my clients want a proposal or a game plan, they want it yesterday. Regular mail takes too much time, and I don't want to use overnight delivery for every document. The price would just be sky-high."
>
> *You:* "I see. I also notice, though, that you have a pretty sophisticated computer system here. Why not just e-mail your clients?"
>
> *Rachel:* "You know, that was the game plan. And the vast majority of my clients actually have e-mail, but they're funny about using it. I work with a lot of small-business owners who've been in operation for the last 300 years. They tend to resist new technology. They don't trust it. Also, they don't like going through the hassle of having to print the information. They don't like information e-mailed, they like it mailed or faxed. They want hard copy in front of them."

You: "Rachel, if you don't mind my saying, it sounds as if you'd choose e-mail over fax if you could, wouldn't you?"

Rachel: "I sure would. Frankly, I hate fax machines. All that fiddling around with buttons, and standing there dealing with paper jams. And by the way, don't try to sell me some state-of-the-art machine. I want a cheapie. It only has to last for two years, three years at the absolute outside. I'm sure that by then e-mail will be so prevalent that fax machines will have gone the way of manual typewriters."

You: "Okay. Let me ask you one other question. What special features are you looking for in a fax machine?"

Rachel: "What do you mean?"

You: "Well, is speed dialing important to you? You know, so you don't have to keep plugging in the fax numbers of your most important clients? A lot of my clients find that a real time-saver. Other clients enjoy being able to use their machines for light photocopying. There's also call-back features, in case a fax line is busy."

Rachel: "No, I have a photocopier, and I'm not going to spend any extra money for a fax machine to do that. Speed dial and call back might be nice, though. Depending on what they cost."

What has the salesman learned thus far?

He has learned that Rachel's actual needs differ from her stated needs.

Rachel's stated need is "a fax machine."

However, she really dislikes fax machines, and in fact, she doesn't need one. She only needs the ability for instant, hard-copy communication with her clients.

The salesman now links a product in his line to her true needs: a means of instant hard-copy communication, rather than the fax machine she says she wants.

You: "So, Rachel, from what you've told me, you want instant, hard-copy communication with your clients, but you really don't like fax machines,

is that right?"

Rachel: "Yup. That's true."

You: "Well I suggest you not invest in a fax machine, per se. I think you might be happier with our ElectroFax software program. It allows you to send and receive faxes from your computer. No need for a separate machine. It sounds as if that would better suit your needs, doesn't it?"

Rachel (leaning forward): "Sure does. Tell me more."

You: "OK! The ElectroFax software program allows you to send and receive faxes via the modem on your computer. A hard copy of the document sent shows up on the receiver's fax machine. However, you can program your computer so that any faxes you receive show up directly on your computer screen...."

In the above scenario, the salesperson has successfully matched a product to his prospect's needs. Rachel was very sure of what she wanted when she called him—but she was incorrectly sure. She thought she needed a traditional fax machine because she was unaware of the electronic options available to her. The salesman, by using strategic questioning, uncovered her true business needs and linked his product to them.

Overcome Objections

We can't afford it.

I need to get more quotes.

It's too expensive.

It's a rare prospect who doesn't initially pose at least some objection to your product, your service, yourself, or your company. If you allow objections to stymie you, you've all but killed your career in sales.

Think about it. If virtually every prospect objects to something about your product, most of your presentations will run this way.

Don't Tell the Yes Guy What His "Problem" Is: Casual Words Can Insult

"You know what your problem is? Your employees just aren't efficient enough."

Say this to a prospect, and you've insulted him. He considers himself a good manager, a sound business owner, and you've just shot down his own best self-perceptions.

It's much better to say, "If I understand you correctly, sir, your current business concerns are...." Or, "Your business needs are...."

Some words invoke trust, others insult.

In this book, we've talked a lot about helping your prospects and clients. It's fine to say to your client, "Ms. Harrison, I think I can help." It's fine to say it once, or maybe even twice. It's not fine to use the word over, and over, and over. Your client may welcome a little help. She will not welcome being made to feel as if she's unable to manage her own affairs, and desperately needs your aid.

During your contacts with prospects and clients, be careful which words you choose. You want to get them excited about your product or service. You don't want an offhand comment to insult them.

Prospect: "We can't afford it."

You: "Thank you for your time, anyway."

Or:

Prospect: "I'll think about it."

You: "Great! I look forward to hearing from you."

Or:

Prospect: "I need to get more quotes."

You: "I understand. Call me when you're done."

Such ready acceptance of a client's protests makes for a pretty short presentation.

And make no mistake: phrases such as "I'll think about it" and "I have to get more quotes" may seem innocuous enough, on their face. But what the prospect really means is "I'm not going to buy your product."

To be a successful salesman, you must learn to overcome a prospect's objections. This does not mean you will clinch every sale. Sometimes, you will prove unable to overcome his worries. But, with a little study, you can learn the techniques to help you uncover the real concerns lurking behind every boilerplate objection.

In fact, you'll learn to look upon objections as a gift. Without objections, it's almost impossible to sell. An objection lets you learn what the prospect is truly concerned about. You deal with objections by validating them and then answering them.

Here's how it works.

Mentally ask the question, "Why?" after every objection posed.

"We can't afford it."

Why can't the prospect afford it? Can he not afford a $3,000 purchase in one lump sum this month? Maybe. And maybe you can offer him an installment plan.

Can he not afford it because he's uncomfortable with your product or service, and uses this phrase just to blow you off? Maybe. Then you can spend some more time outlining the benefits of your product and service, until he understands it well enough to feel comfortable investing.

Can he not afford it because his buying power in the company caps at $10,000, and your product runs $12,000? You can either rewrite a contract for two $6,000 purchases, or take your current prospect with you as you find the true Yes Guy—the person with both the need for your product, and buying power in excess of $12,000.

Think of objections as a request for more information. A prospect who says he can't afford it may really be begging you to find a way for him to afford it. An "I'll think about it" may mean that you've not been entirely successful in linking your product to your prospect's needs. "I need to get other quotes" means that the prospect does not yet understand the value of your product or service.

Like other sales scenarios, overcoming objections follows a certain general formula.

- You listen to your prospect's objections. Show you understand his concerns by nodding your head at appropriate times, saying, "I understand," or "I see how you feel."

- You ask questions about his issues. "What do you still need to think about, sir? Is there something I've not explained fully?" Or: "Sir, why do you feel the need to get more quotes? Perhaps I can just take another moment or two to go over your needs, and how my product can fill them."

- Summarize his objections. "So, if I understand you correctly, you can't afford a $3,000 down payment this month?" Or: "So, while you would like to invest in our service, only the company president can sign off on this purchase?"

- Overcome the objections. Accommodate the objection if you can. Break that $3,000 down payment into two $1,500 installments. Enlist the current prospect's help in getting to the true Yes Guy. Link your product to your prospect's needs so thoroughly that he won't see a need to get other quotes.

- Move on. Don't dwell on the objection.

What "I Can't Afford It" Really Means

You represent Aqua Clear, Inc., a company that services and landscapes swimming pools in exclusive apartment complexes. You've presented your services to Rick Smith, Senior VP for Reem Properties, Inc., which operates ten luxury high-rises. The first part of your presentation has gone smoothly, you think. Now Smith poses his objections.

> *Rick:* "Look, I've seen your work at other complexes. The gardens you plant are lovely, they're always well-kept, and the pool water is terrifically clean. But $100,000 a year? That's too expensive."

> *You:* "I see. Can I ask exactly what you mean by 'too expensive'? "(This can be: He doesn't feel like spending that much money, you're more expensive than your competition, he just doesn't have the money up front, or he doesn't have the buying power to OK this purchase.)

> *Rick:* "Our current pool guy only charges us $82,000 per year. I don't see how I can justify an additional $18,000."

> *You:* "I understand. Rick, let me ask you: Are you satisfied with your current pool maintenance company?" (Of course he's not. If he were, he wouldn't be meeting with you.)

> *Rick:* "No. They keep the chlorine balance all right, but they're not always so great with the gardens. Leaves sometimes blow into the pool, and our tenants get upset. They're paying prime rents, and they don't like sloppiness. So I keep talking to the boss over there, and he yesses me to death, but he doesn't respond. And then the tenants keep calling. Some of them are really mad. Now, on top of that, we're finding discoloration at the bottom of some of the pools. Under contract, our current pool guy is supposed to sand blast, but the company only gets around to it when they…get around to it."

> *You:* "Do you ever fear that tenants will move out because of the situation?"

Rick: "Yeah. Yeah, I do."

You: "And what does your average rental go for?"

Rick: "$2,000 per month."

You: "OK, Rick. Let's look at it this way. Each of your tenants pays you $24,000 per year. And you know the value of good tenants; they can be very hard to replace. So keeping just one tenant would more than pay for the extra $18,000, wouldn't it?"

Rick: "Yeah, I guess I see your point."

You: "Terrific. Now, as I was saying, we can write the paperwork so that our service begins mid-month or on the first of the month. Which would you prefer?"

(Notice how the salesman quickly moves on after he has satisfied the objection.)

In this scenario, the salesman expertly moved the conversation from price and toward value. Rick originally thought Aqua Clear to be too expensive, because it ran $18,000 per year more than his current service. The salesman, however, showed Rick that he simply could not afford to keep his current pool-maintenance company. Sticking with the same-old same-old would result in a loss of valuable rental income.

But, as noted above, "I can't afford it" can mean a variety of things to a variety of people. Since this is perhaps the most common objection, it's best to review that oblique phrase's other meanings.

Rick: "Look, I've seen your work at other complexes. The gardens you plant are lovely, they're always well-kept, and the pool water is terrifically clean. But $100,000 a year? That's too expensive. I can't afford it."

You: "I see. Can I ask exactly what you mean by 'too expensive'?"

Rick: "Well, we'd want to start with a new service mid-year, meaning June 1. And traditionally, the second half of the year is 'leaner' for us than the first. So we only have $40,000 to spend on pool services through the end of the year."

You: "I certainly understand that, and I think I can help. When you use our

service, we can arrange things so that you invest $40,000 during the last six months of this year, and $60,000 during the first six months of next year. That would take care of your budget concerns, wouldn't it?"

Your prospect may also say a product is too expensive because the investment falls beyond the bounds of his purchasing authority. You have two options in such a situation: You can break your payment into installments that he can personally OK, or you can enlist his support in selling to the true Yes Guy.

Here are some examples:

> *Rick:* "I really like your work, and I'd love to hire you, but $100,000 is just too expensive. I can't sign off on that."
>
> *You:* "Rick, I really appreciate your interest. And I think our service could help Reem Properties. It sounds like you'd like to hire us, wouldn't you?"
>
> *Rick:* "Yeah, I would. But I can only OK purchases of $85,000 or less."
>
> *You:* "Rick, how about if I break our service into two separate items— $50,000 for pool care, and $50,000 for garden maintenance? Would you be able to OK those investments?"
>
> *Rick:* "Yes, I can!"
>
> *You:* "Terrific! Now let's talk about a maintenance schedule...."

Or:

> *Rick:* "I really like your work, and I'd love to hire you, but $100,000 is just too expensive. I can't sign off on that."
>
> *You:* "Rick, I really appreciate your interest. And I think our service could help Reem Properties. It sounds like you'd like to hire us, wouldn't you?"
>
> *Rick:* "Yeah, I would. But our owner, Will Reem, told me that if a pool-maintenance service costs a penny over $82,000, it has to go through him."
>
> *You:* "All right, then. Why don't you and I set up a meeting to meet with Mr. Reem? Would Tuesday or Thursday be better?"

Information, Please

Never leave a presentation with a prospect simply promising to "think about it." Frankly, once you leave his office, he won't have to think about your product or service, and therefore, he won't. And you've most likely lost a sale.

Even a firm "No, thanks. We just don't want it" is far better for the salesman, psychologically, than an "I'll think about it and get back to you." You know how to deal with "no." You know how to soldier on in the face of rejection. (Or you will, after reading chapter 11.) But a promise to consider your proposal leaves you in a state of limbo. Should you keep trying to sell the prospect? Should you write him off?

You save yourself a lot of angst by strongly working toward some type of advancement before you leave the room—a close, another meeting, a no, anything but "I'll think about it."

While "I'll think about it" may not, strictly speaking, be an objection, it is the blanket phrase that people most often use to indicate they have objections, but they have not yet spent the time to formulate them.

Force your prospect to express his true concerns. Chances are, once he actually states his objections, you can overcome them.

In the following scenario, you represent Regional Polling Services Inc., a marketing firm that conducts straw polls for politicians. You've met with Leo Roberts, campaign manager for a Democratic Congressional primary candidate. You've explained your service, and aim for the close. Then Leo pipes up with:

> *Leo:* "Well, thanks a lot for your time. Let me think about it and I'll get back to you."
>
> *You:* "And thank you for your time, Leo. Before I leave, let me just ask— what do you need to think about? Have I been unclear?"
>
> *Leo:* "No, not unclear, exactly. You quoted me a price of $13,000, plus phone charges. You're asking $7,000 for your report and game plan. That I understand. But you've also included 30 people each working for 20 hours at $10 per hour. That's another $6,000. I'm thinking "Why don't I

just get 30 volunteers in here to do the polling for free?"

You: "I understand your concerns, Leo. And clearly, saving as much money as you can is important in the early stages of any campaign. But you want as accurate results as possible from this poll, don't you?"

Leo: "Of course I do. Why would I even want to conduct an inaccurate poll?"

You: "You wouldn't. No one would. Leo, let me tell you something, I have the utmost respect for anyone who takes time out of his schedule to volunteer for a cause he believes in. But there's a clear skill to telephone polling. You have to read off a script but sound as if you're not reading from a script. You have to be able to soldier on in the face of hang-ups. It's tough. Some volunteers are so dedicated to a candidate that they don't want to seem as if they're doing a bad job. They get embarrassed if they receive too many hang-ups, and they just start answering the questions themselves. Regional Polling has a staff of 100 fully trained on-call professionals. They know how to keep calling no matter how many rude responses they get. They don't take it personally. Frankly, in our experience, they just get 'truer' responses than volunteers do."

In this scenario, by asking the prospect why he still had to think about, the salesman has uncovered the prospect's true objections: he was not convinced of the worth of the salesman's service. The salesman was then able to overcome that objection by helping the prospect understand the value of trained telemarketers.

Somebody Out There Doesn't Like You

You know the Nixon-era joke: Just because you're paranoid, it doesn't mean they're not out to get you.

New salesmen often suffer from bouts of low self-confidence. They're afraid that prospects won't like them.

And some prospects won't.

They probably won't dislike you, as a person, but they may have heard less than great things about your company. Even the soundest, most reputable companies and salespeople screw up sometimes.

So, your presentation has gone well, but, as you go for the close, the prospect says something innocuous, probably something like, "I just don't know. I have to think about it."

> *You:* "Sir, can I ask what it is you still need to think about? Is there something I still need to explain?"
>
> *Prospect:* "No. It's just that, I gotta tell you. I used to work over at Levine & James. This was about six years ago, and one of your office supply guys really messed us over. It was tax time, we needed 2,000 binders to put all these tax returns in, and hand out to our clients. What do we get a week before tax day? Two thousand staplers. Now, I understand that mistakes happen, I've made more than a few myself. But when I called the salesman to tell him he said, "Oh. Let me get to work on that." Period, end of story. No apologies, no offer of a price break. I just took my business elsewhere. I don't know. I like you, I like your products. I just don't know if I can trust your company again."

How do you overcome this problem? You tell the prospect that, despite bad experiences with other salespeople in your company, you're the one he'll be working with now.

> *You:* "Sir, I understand your concern, and I'm very, very sorry that this mix-up happened to you. I'm even more sorry that the salesman seemed unconcerned about the effect his mistake had on your businesses. I can only tell you this: If you decide to contract with Pens Office Supplies, you'll be dealing with me. I work hard to satisfy each of my customers, but you can bet, if I ever do make a mistake, I'll rectify it immediately."

Grabbing 'Em with Sales Aids

People can talk forever. Listening is a little harder. The prospect can babble on and on. He won't listen half that long.

Human attention span is short. You need to sell through concisely worded phrases, and through sales aids.

Sales aids can help keep your clients' attention. They can help you get to his side of the desk, and begin working as a team.

However, no brochure, no beautifully prepared press package, no clearly drawn chart, ever sold anything. Only you can do that.

In fact, sales aids can actually hinder the process. When it comes time for you to speak, you want to be sure that the prospect's attention rests on you, not on the latest wonders of your company's latest product, as outlined in your sales brochure. You want him listening, not reading.

Be careful of when you choose to use sales aids. Allow them to only enhance what you're saying. Don't let them overshadow your words.

Handing a prospect a chart, getting to his side of the desk, and saying, "Well, Mr. Jones, as you can see from my research, my service will likely save you about $5,000 a year," is fine.

Don't willy-nilly hand your prospect that same chart, and then begin your little spiel linking your product to his needs. He won't be paying attention to you—he'll be reading the chart.

Demo products, if not used correctly, can also hurt rather than enhance your chances of making the sale.

Suppose you sell a high-tech gadget. You stick it on the desk at the beginning of your presentation. The client will not express his needs; he will not listen to your input. He will play with the gadget. And maybe he won't know how to use it. So instead of speaking and hearing, he sits there, playing with this thing, becoming increasingly frustrated at his inability to operate it.

You've lost a lot here. You've lost your opportunity to uncover the prospect's needs. You've lost your chance to link your product to those needs. And you've lost his faith in your product.

The Hazards of Showing up Late, or Too Early

Clearly, you respect your prospect's time. If you have been allotted a 12:30 p.m. appointment, you don't show up at 1:00.

You leave your office a few minutes early to make sure you get to the meeting on time. If your prospect works in a section of town that you're not familiar with, you may take a "test drive" in advance of the appointment, just to be sure you know the way.

This is only common sense. You respect your client's time, and you will do everything in your power to avoid showing up late.

But what if you show up too early?

This is a peril as well. Showing up too early makes you look inappropriately eager. It makes you look as if you have time to waste hanging out in anterooms and reception areas. And a salesman with lots of extra time on his hands can't be too great a salesman.

Arrive for your appointment five or ten minutes early, no more. If you find yourself in the parking lot 20 minutes before your scheduled appointment, relax a bit. Listen to the radio. Or take a short walk to clear your head.

Enter your prospect's reception area five or ten minutes before your appointment. Announce yourself to the receptionist. Use the intervening time to look around a bit. Peruse any materials left for visitors. Pick up any subtle clues about the business.

Relax, and get ready for your presentation.

Instead, demonstrate your products like this:

Wait until you've asked your strategic questions. Wait until you've uncovered his needs. Wait until you've linked your products to those needs. Then say something like, "Mr. Ward, let me take a moment to show you how it works."

Put the gadget on his desk, and gently guide him through its operation. Reassure him and compliment him often. "Hey, you're doing great!" "You're really picking up on this quickly!"

Then this is what you've gained: Your client has spoken. You've listened. You've talked. He has listened. Then, by leading your prospect through a demo of your product, you've instilled in him the same enthusiasm that you feel.

And you've won a sale.

If You Honestly Can't Help

Sometimes, despite all your prospecting work, you will end a presentation realizing that you've just spent a half-hour with a potential client you honestly can't help.

You sell $50,000 power boats; your client is looking for a kayak, and can't afford much more. You sell Louis XIV furniture, and your prospect is looking to outfit the kid's playroom. You breed German shepherds, and your prospect and her family have definitely decided they want a golden retriever.

What do you do in these situations?

Walk away. Your willingness to walk away rather than to push a prospect into a product or service he doesn't need or want is perhaps the best demonstration of your integrity.

How do you walk?

Say this:

"Ma'am, I'm sorry to have taken up your time unnecessarily, but, after speaking with you for a bit, I realize I don't have the type of product you're looking for. Let me tell you something, though—I know who might. The people at X Company offer what you want. I have a friend there, let me give you his name and number."

Yes, you are turning your prospect over to a competitor—but a competitor who offers a product or service that you can't.

Your prospect will be amazed by your honesty. She will really appreciate it. She's not expecting a salesperson to be this up front.

She'll be impressed.

And you can take great advantage—in the best sense of the word—of her impression. You can ask her for referrals, using the techniques described in chapter 4.

You'll lose this one sale, but because of your honesty and integrity, you'll get a slew of referrals.

THE Close

The training wheels have come off the bike, and the child wobbles, trying to get his sense of balance. Mom or Dad holds onto the seat, steadying the bike so the boy won't fall, jogging alongside as he pedals.

And the kid keeps yelling, "Ya got me, right? Ya got me?!"

And the parent says, "Yup. Right here. I got you."

But after some time—depending on the child's ability, maybe a few hours, a few days, or a few weeks—the parent will quietly let go. The kid will be yelling, "Ya got me, right?" for 100 yards before he realizes he's pedaling on his own. An amazing thing:

most children don't fall. They get scared for a millisecond, but their fears melt away under the exhilaration of actually riding a bike on their own.

The kid needed the push. He will never, ever say, "It's OK to let go now, Mommy. I am completely confident of my ability to ride this bike." He has an inherent fear of saying "yes." Had the parent not let go, one day you'd see a 35-year-old riding around with his 65-year-old parent jogging alongside.

The Close.

The trickiest moment in any presentation is the time when a prospect commits to investing in your product or service, commits to buying, commits to evolving into a client.

Closing, at heart, is the process through which a salesperson helps a prospect overcome the inherent fear of saying "yes." And usually, like the kid on the bike, the prospect will need a push.

This does not mean you use gimmicks. This does not mean you become a stereotypical, glad-handing salesman.

As the old ideas of sales practices—slap 'em on the back and sell 'em, regardless of whether they need your goods—fall by the wayside, closing evolves into reaching agreement. Your prospect has reached a point where he wants to invest, and you want to sell—because you truly believe that your product or service will help fill his needs.

Your belief in your ability to help your prospect should permeate the sales process, from the moment you decide to accept a job. Ally yourself with a reputable product and company, develop a list of prospects who truly need your product or service, hone cold-calling techniques to help you find the true Yes Guy and get an appointment, spend time on your pre-call planning to determine which of your products or services will best help a prospect, ask strategic questions, link your goods to a prospect's needs, and overcome inevitable objections.

Voilà! Instant sale?

Not quite. Invariably, no matter how terrific your work, the prospect will need a push before investing. He will need you to help him overcome his fear of saying "yes." Remember, people want. They just don't like to pay.

Prepare for the close before you walk in the door. Here's how:

- Develop a "Yes" mind-set. Psyche yourself up for the close with your belief in your ability to help your prospect. This belief should permeate your attitude. You should exude confidence. Learn to phrase your statements to reflect this mind-set. You should always say, "When you invest in our service," rather than "If you invest in our service." Or, "When we deliver our product," rather than "If you want our product, we'll be able to deliver it as soon as you like."

- Expand on the similar situation. Remember the hot buttons that got you the appointment? The direct referrals or the companies, similar to your prospect's, that have invested in your product or service? Take a few moments now to write up a few paragraphs describing these situations. (Depending on how specifically you speak about another client's business, you may need to call him first to get his OK.) While cold calling, it's fine to say, "We've been able to help other businesses like yours, including Thompson & Associates, save overtime pay during peak work periods by employing our temporary workers."

In your presentation, particularly as you near the close, prepare to get much more specific.

You may want to write up something like this:

In 1996, Thompson & Associates Accounting spent $15,000 during tax season to pay its secretaries overtime. The overtime was mandatory, and the firm lost some of its best support people to burnout. In 1997, Mr. Thompson decided to contract with Minute Temps. He gave his staff secretaries the overtime they wanted—about $5,000 worth. He used Minute Temps for the rest of the work—investing a total of $8,000. As a result, Thompson & Associates filed timely returns for all its clients for $2,000 less than the firm had spent in 1996, and without any employee burnout.

- Plan the outcome. Assume the prospect will invest with you, and fill out an implementation schedule or order form before you walk in the door for your presentation. This shows the client how enthusiastic you are, and also indicates that you have already invested time in him. This "investment" will make it harder for him to say no.

Leave specific dates blank. Ask the prospect to help you fill them in.

It works like this:

> *You*: "So, Mr. Alamos, from what we've said, you need a painter who will pressure-wash your house, and apply a base coat and a top coat by the day of your family reunion, is that correct?"

> *Alamos:* "Sure is. I just bought this house, and I'm proud of it. I want to show off a little."

> *You :* "And you should. It's a beautiful home, and I think the colors we discussed will really look terrific. Let's talk about how we can accomplish what you want."

At this point, you remove a work plan from your briefcase. It reads something like this: Ready Paint, Inc. Work Plan

Prepared For: Mr. Harold Alamos

Pressure Washing Completion Date:

Base Coat Completion Date:

Top Coat Completion Date:

> *You:* "OK, Mr. Alamos. I want your house to look terrific by the time your relatives visit. So let's figure out how we can do it. Will you help me fill in these dates?"

> *Alamos:* "OK."

> *You:* "I suggest that my employees start pressure-washing your home on May 15. Is that OK with you?"

Alamos: "Sure."

You: "Terrific. On May 19, they'll begin with the base coat. This will take two full days, plus one day for it to dry. That brings us to the 21st. Is that all right?"

Alamos (nodding): "Yeah."

You: "Great. Then on May 22, we begin with the top coat, which we'll complete by the 27th, well before your relatives start showing up on June 15."

Alamos: "This sounds great, but what if it rains?"

You: "That's why I've left a three-week time cushion."

Alamos: "Good thinking."

(Note: You should fill in the dates on your work plan/order form as the prospect agrees to each.)

This will not work every single time. Some of your action plans and order forms will end up in the circular file. But filling out an order form ahead of time will serve as a measure of your confidence, and make your product more difficult for the prospect to resist.

Buying Time

Don't guess about when your prospect is ready to buy. Let him tell you himself.

Now, he probably won't pop up with, "I'm just dying to sign the contract." That would be too easy. Instead, he'll give you a number of verbal and nonverbal signals.

Nonverbal signals include leaning forward in his chair and nodding his head, and looking at you more and more intently.

Verbal buying signals include saying, "Boy, that sounds good," or "Terrific," or "Wow." Some of his questions, such as, "Would you be able to start your service by Thursday?" or "When could you deliver the product?" also indicate strong interest.

Finally, even objections—notably picayune objections—can serve as buying signals.

If a prospect says to you, "Your game plan here indicates that you'll install my new computer at two o'clock on Monday. That's no good for me. A lot of customers call in the later afternoon," he's grasping at anything to quibble over. This means that, in his heart, he wants you to convince him to buy your product or service.

All you need to do is install the computer at noon, when the switchboard shuts down for the lunch hour.

Tried-and-True Closes

Here comes the push we discussed earlier in the chapter. Remember, there is nothing wrong with pushing a bit. All you do, in any of the closes listed below, is help your prospect overcome his inherent fear of saying yes.

Choice of Alternatives

This close takes the same form as the multiple-choice question examined in chapter 7. You do not ask someone whether he wants to buy your product or service. Remember, if you give a prospect a choice between yes or no, he will pick no virtually every time. Instead, offer him a choice between Product A or Product B. Chances are, he will pick either A or B.

Here's how it works:

> *You:* "So, Mr. Bunker. As discussed, you're looking for an air conditioner to cool a 400-square-foot room, is that correct?"
>
> *Bunker:* "Yes."
>
> *You:* "OK. I have two options for you. The SuperCool 1000, which has an energy-efficiency rating of 9. The SuperCool 1000B has the same cooling power and energy efficiency, and also has an air-cleaning feature that helps remove spores and mold from your home. Which would you prefer?"

Never Say "Sold" and Other Dirty Words

Imagine a salesman saying to a prospect, "If you let me sell you this product, well…you'll be spending a whole lot of money, but I can guarantee that after we sign the contract and you accept delivery, you'll see a quick return."

You couldn't think of a better way to frighten him, short of jumping out from beneath a tree one dark night, shouting "BOO!"

Some words will invoke fear in your prospect, others trust and enthusiasm. A successful salesperson, while never telling less than the truth, knows which words to use to set a prospect at ease.

Here are some examples:

Buy: Substitute "invest" or "own." As in, "When you invest in our service," or, "When you own our product."

Sell: Use "help" or "worked with." Don't say, "After I sold a new computer to Will Picard, he really noticed an increase in his overall work efficiency." Say instead, "I was able to help Will Picard increase his work efficiency."

Contract: Instead, use "paperwork" or "agreement." Don't say, "It's time to sign the contract now." But rather, "Let's look over the paperwork."

The Balance Sheet

In this close, you help your prospect list the benefits and drawbacks of investing in your product or service. If you've done your job right from the beginning, the positives should so far outweigh the negatives that your prospect has, psychologically, no choice but to invest.

It works like this.

You represent the Big Blue Bus, a service that provides chauffeured bus and limousine transportation to private functions. You've met with Sarah Lawrence, the mother of a soon-to-be bride. She is considering using your service for her out-of-town guests, to deliver them to her daughter's wedding, to the reception, then back to their hotels. You've done your work well, understanding her need for this service and linking your service to this need. Still, she's on the fence. Her objections keep shifting. You no sooner overcome one than she presents another. Finally, she admits:

> *Sarah:* "Look, I don't know what's wrong. I just can't make up my mind."
>
> *You:* "I understand this is a big decision for you, Sarah. And I think I can help."

At this point, you take a piece of paper out of your briefcase. On one side, you write the word "Yes." On the other side, "No."

> *You:* "It might help you make a decision if we write down the pros and cons of investing in our service. Would that be all right?"
>
> *Sarah (nodding):* "Fine, yeah."
>
> *You:* "Great. OK. Now, as we discussed, contracting with our service provides you with safe transport for your guests to and from the wedding reception. It's not unusual for someone to have an extra drink at a happy occasion like this, and you don't want any tipsy drivers, right?"
>
> *Sarah:* "Right."
>
> *You:* "OK."

You write down this positive, and all the following, in the "Yes" column.

Nobody Ever Got Rich Cutting Prices

At the close, your prospect may start making noises about how much he likes your product or service, but finds it a little too expensive.

Many salespeople, especially new salespeople, will immediately offer to cut their prices.

Resist this temptation. Resist it for two reasons. First, your willingness to drop your price indicates (usually wrongly) a lack of faith in your product. How can a prospect believe in its worth if you don't?

Second, and—from a selfish point of view—more important, giving a client a price break may mean eating into your own commission.

Nobody ever got rich cutting prices.

Instead, you need to figure out exactly what the prospect means by too expensive (examined in chapter 8). In all likelihood, the prospect has made this statement at this time because you have not yet helped him understand, for himself, the worth of your product or service. Backtrack a bit, again linking your product to your prospect's needs, and help him to understand its value.

You: "Also, we've talked about the overall success of the wedding. With the bus service, you won't have any stragglers walking down the aisle after the bride. Finally, there's convenience. You don't want to have all your relatives renting cars to get to the big event. This just about covers the reasons to invest in our service, doesn't it?"

Sarah: "Yes, it does."

You: "Great! So off the top of our heads, here's what's in the plus column. *(At this point, you turn your paper over to Sarah.)* Safety, convenience, and overall conduct of the wedding. Now, why don't you tell me what the negatives are?"

Thus far, you've helped your prospect determine the "pluses" of your product or service. But don't shoot yourself in the foot here. Don't help her determine the negatives.

Your prospect may respond with, "I don't really see any negatives." At that point, don't pause. Go for the sale, usually offering a multiple-choice option. But suppose she takes a hard look at the balance sheet, and comes up with another objection? At least she will have spent a few minutes thinking about the matter, and her objection will more likely prove a concrete one—one you can overcome.

The Obligating Close

In chapter 7, we talked about the obligating question—a promise made on your part to perform work IF the prospect agrees that, upon its completion, he will advance the sale.

Obligating questions, in and of themselves, often serve as a closing technique.

Here's how.

You represent Photo Finish, a manufacturer of upscale picture frames. You want your wares stocked in Lickety Split Pix, a chain of photo developers. You near the end of your presentation, and sales VP Bud Marx says:

Bud: "I really like the samples you've shown, but I don't see anything with a bunny motif. Easter's just a month away, and that's what I'm worrying about now—bunnies. All these parents want to put pictures of their kids in bunny frames to send off to the grandparents."

You: "Bud, how many bunny frames can you use?"

Bud: "Two hundred thousand, nationwide."

You: "OK, Bud. If I promise to get 200,000 bunny frames to your warehouse by Thursday, will you stock a full line of Photo Finish frames in your stores, as discussed?"

Bud: "Yeah. Yeah, I will."

You: "Terrific."

Take out your order form (previously filled in) and amend it to include the bunny frames.

The Similar Situation Close

All those hot buttons that helped you get a meeting can now help you close the sale. As discussed above, the presentation isn't the time to say, "We've been able to help several companies like yours, including Harry Smith Industries, increase employee productivity, and avoid burnout by investing in our service." The close is the time to prove it.

Call your current client. Ask whether you can use her as a reference. Then take some time to write and print out a case study detailing all you've done for that business. Keep the sheet in your briefcase, to use at the appropriate time.

In the following scenario, you represent the Las Rojas, a Yellow Pages–like telephone directory that targets Hispanic businesses, and is then delivered to Hispanic households.

You've called upon Emmanuel Rodriguez, the owner of Rodriguez Hardware & Lumber.

You: "So, as you see, Mr. Rodriguez, our research indicates that many Hispanic people prefer to patronize Hispanic-owned businesses. The problem is finding them. Our book fills that need. Every single business listed inside it is owned or operated by Spanish-speaking people. And we deliver only to Hispanic households. We don't try to reach every household on the block, only Hispanic households. That way, we keep our prices down, and you see a terrific return on a very reasonable investment."

Emmanuel: "I can see the potential, but this is a small business. You're asking for $5,000. You say that many of your clients can trace increased business to that investment. But I just can't be sure."

You (taking a prepared similar-situation scenario from your briefcase): "I think I can help you be sure, sir. This is a history of what we've done for Rosa's Florists. As you can see, her business income has increased by $12,000 a year over the last two years. She's not running her shops any differently: She has the same number of employees, the same two locations. The only difference she's made over the last two years is her investment in Las Rojas. She's seen a $24,000 return on a $10,000 investment."

Emmanuel (looking over the sheet): "This looks wonderful. But I..."

You: "Would you like me to call Rosa for you right now? We can confirm these figures...."

The Puppy Dog

This can prove the most devastating close of all. It allows your prospect to try out a product or service for a given period of time—paying very little or nothing for the privilege—before determining whether he wants to keep it.

Why do you think so many automobile dealers offer incentives for simply test-driving a car? You've heard the ads. "In the market for a luxury automobile? Drop by Angstrom Mercedes. Take one of our sleek machines for a spin, and we'll give you 100 dollars."

Angstrom knows he will hand out a few Ben Franklins to people who can't even afford a Hyundai, but who've spotted a way to make a few easy bucks. But his deeper knowledge says this: Most people who swing by will actually be in the market for a luxury car. And once they drive a Mercedes, feel the leather, run their fingers along the polished wood of the dash, listen to Sinatra crooning from eight perfectly positioned speakers, and roll down the sunroof, the car will become theirs. They won't want to let it go.

You can learn a lot from Angstrom.

If you're selling a revolutionary new type of software, and your prospect sits on the fence, let him try it out for a week or two—for free. If it's as good as you think, he'll have grown to love it by then. He will not call you to ask to have it uninstalled. Rather, you'll call him, meet with him, and walk away with a contract.

"Today's Special," "Last Chance," and When to Use Them

"At Frane's Furniture, this week only, all prices on leather sectional sofas have been slashed 50 percent. That's right! 50 percent! Leather sectionals in blue, black, brown, or white, not $1,500, not $1,250, not $1,000, but only $750!"

If you were sitting at home one night and saw this commercial on TV, would it make you want to run out to Frane's?

Maybe, maybe not.

The commercial might whet your appetite if you happen to be in the market for leather sectional sofas.

If you're happy with your current furniture, or you want new furniture but you hate leather because of the way it sticks to your skin in the summer heat, you'll probably just reach for the remote.

So, how will the use of special offers assist you in making sales?

Certainly not by walking into a presentation screaming, "Today's special! One week only! Prices slashed! Incentives Galore!" Your prospect won't care, because he has not yet discovered, for himself, the value of your product or service.

As any good shopper knows, if it doesn't look good on you, if it won't wear or wash well, if it doesn't serve your needs, or if you just plain don't want it—it's not a bargain, no matter how inexpensive.

It's not that a special offer can't prove a very effective closing tool. You just don't want to base your presentation on it. Instead, use special offers once a prospect has pretty much made up his mind to invest, but needs a little extra nudge.

Closing a sale, like asking questions, is a fluid process. Don't expect that you'll walk in, use the Balance Sheet, and walk out with a sale. It won't always work that way. You may have to combine closes. If a Balance Sheet doesn't work, try the Puppy Dog. If your Obligating Close doesn't work, transition to a Balance Sheet.

If You've Blown It: Dealing with Someone Who Is Unable to Give You a Yes

In chapter 5, you read about the perils of selling to someone who can only say no. You've worked hard to find the Yes Guy. But sometimes, at this late stage, you'll realize that you've made a mistake. That, despite all your research, you've blown it— delivering your presentation to someone who can't approve the purchase.

If you didn't discover your mistake earlier in the sales process, you'll certainly learn of it when you go for the close.

The prospect won't let you close.

He'll raise an objection. You'll overcome it. He'll raise another. You'll overcome it. Then his objections will start to shift, becoming increasingly nebulous.

You need to narrow the conversation and get your prospect to either focus or confess that he is not the Yes Guy.

Once he 'fesses up, you'll have several options. You can determine his purchasing authority and try to arrange payment for your product or service in terms that he can OK, you can enlist him as an aid to help you influence the true Yes Guy, or you can go over his head.

The Puppy Dog Close Works Even with Puppies

(or, Why a Tryout Can Bring You Big Bucks)

How did the Puppy Dog Close get its name?

Consider this:

A man wants to buy a male golden retriever, but he fails to make this clear to the breeder during their telephone conversations. He visits the breeder planning to buy; the only problem is, the breeder has no males available.

"Sorry about that," the breeder says. "Let me make a few telephone calls to see if there are any available males around. In the meantime, would you just hold this puppy for a minute or two?"

The breeder hands her prospect a fat, happy, female golden, and the prospect begins to play with her.

After 45 minutes on the phone, the breeder re-enters the room. "Sir," she says, "I'm sorry for the confusion. We can have a male golden for you by Monday. And since we seem to have gotten our lines crossed a bit, we'll be happy to deliver him to your house. No extra charge. How would that be?"

Prospect: "I don't want a male. I want this one."

Think the breeder is shocked? Of course not. Once someone bonds with a puppy, it's very hard to let go.

Of all the closes you can learn, the Puppy Dog is perhaps the most powerful.

You probably don't sell puppies. You probably tout much less adorable products or services. But the premise remains the same: Once a prospect has "bonded" with your wares, enjoyed a free tryout of your product or service, he won't want to let go. And you've clinched a sale.

At the very least, try to get the name of the true Yes Guy before leaving this presentation.

In the following scenario, you represent RapidTalk communications systems. You've called on a large regional business, and believe you can help lower its monthly telephone bills. Your service requires a $10 per month fee for each line—$1,200 per month for this 120-person company, or $14,400 per year. The presentation has gone well, but your prospect's objections have grown more and more nebulous. At this point, you need to pin down the prospect, saying, as diplomatically as possible, something like this:

> *You:* "Mr. Sands, you've had a lot of questions about RapidTalk, and I've done my best to answer them. But frankly, I feel as though I'm not doing my job very well today, because clearly, I've not answered all your concerns. I feel bad because I know that RapidTalk would help your company reduce those phone bills. It would really help me to help you if you'd just take a second to think about what your most serious concerns are, and then tell me. Would you do that, please?"

Then shut up.

Your prospect may end up being honest with you. If he lacks a $14,400 purchasing authority, your conversation may run this way:

> *Mr. Sands:* "Look, no. I think this a great service, but I can only OK purchases up to $10,000. I'm just wondering how I can get the president to sign off on this."
>
> *You:* "Mr. Sands, would it help if I broke this contract into two, $7,200 purchases, one for the first six months of the year, the other for the last?"

Or you may find that the prospect has no purchasing authority whatsoever:

> *Mr. Sands:* "No, you've explained everything very well. But I don't have any purchasing authority, so I can't sign off on this contract. Only the president of our company can do that."

Now you've uncovered the true problem. Try very hard to enlist Mr. Sands as an ally.

Mr. Sands wants to buy, and his opinion may carry great weight with the true Yes Guy. Say something like the following:

> *You:* "Mr. Sands, I completely understand. Why don't you and I set up a time when we can both meet with the president?"

With any luck, your prospect will agree to the idea. But he may balk. He may tell you that he'll happily report your information to the president. You don't want that. Nobody can possibly care as much about your wares, about your business, as you do. Here, make one more stab at enlisting the No Guy as an aid, diplomatically pointing out why your attendance at the meeting is imperative.

If all else fails, you may have to go over his head.

This is not your first choice. You don't want to insult somebody unnecessarily. If the eventual Yes Guy does, in fact, decide to invest in your product or service, you may have to deal with your initial contact in the future. You'd just as soon the relationship proved a cordial one.

However, if your initial contact proves unwilling to advance the sale, you may have to jump over his head to the true Yes Guy.

How?

Call the Yes Guy. In the above scenario, that would be the corporate president. Say something like:

> *You:* "Hello, sir, this Bill Washington calling from RapidTalk Communications. You may know that I spoke with your vice president, Mr. Sands, a few days ago, about a telephone system that I believe will save your company $10,000 next year. He said I'd have to speak with you about any investment, and I'd like for us to meet. Would Tuesday or Thursday be better for you?"

Knowing When to Shut Up

Simon and Garfunkel sang about the sound of silence. Accomplished salespeople could pen a tune about the power of silence.

Selling often means knowing when to shut up.

Many closes, including the choice of alternatives and the balance sheet, require a moment of silence on your part. After you ask the prospect, "Would you prefer Product A or Product B," or after you've given the prospect the opportunity to fill in the "No" side of your balance sheet, sit there silently.

People don't like quiet. You've noticed this on dates, or at small dinner parties. When a conversation starts to lag, people try hard to think of anything to say to fill the awkward silence.

Let your prospect experience this awkwardness. He may break the silence with an agreement to buy. At the very least, he may use the time to collect his thoughts on any lingering doubts he has about your product or service. He will express them as objections, which you can overcome, and advance the sale.

KEEPING *the sale* and generating *repeat* BUSINESS

Remember how, after your eighth birthday, your mom insisted that you sit down and write thank-you notes to the relatives and friends who'd given you, oh, a 64-box of Crayolas, a Matchbox car, a Barbie doll, and a pair of plaid socks?

It didn't much matter whether you liked the gifts. You had to write the notes.

This was good training. Courtesy separates Homo sapiens from other life forms. But etiquette has its mercenary side. Say Aunt Mabel sent you a $50 check when you turned eight. If you took the time to say thanks, you dramatically increased your chances of getting a similar check at age nine.

Everybody wants acknowledgment for the good they do, the kindness they impart.

Your clients are no different. Thank-you notes and thank-you gifts serve as a sincere expression of your appreciation. Follow-ups and customer care indicate that your client's business or life is truly important to you—important enough to see whether

DROP-INS

You've learned that you should always set a firm appointment to meet with a prospect, rather than stopping by his office and hoping he'll have a few spare minutes to see you.

You can loosen this rule a bit when working in the customer-care arena.

If you enjoy an established relationship with a client, it's fine to drop by for a few minutes to see how well your new product/service is performing; to let your client know about new products or upgrades, to alert him to industry changes, or just to say "hi." While you should still schedule firm appointments for formal presentations, drop-bys can do much to increase your rapport with a client.

your product or service performs as it should. Follow-ups will lead to repeat business and to referrals. Finally, post-sale contact with your client keeps your name and your company's name, in the forefront of his mind. This is discussed thoroughly in chapter 11.

The Art of Saying Thanks

Clearly, you should shake the customer's hand and say thank you at the close of every sale. However, this can be slightly more complicated than it sounds. You have provided your customer with a product or service that you truly believe will fill a need. Therefore, you don't need to fawn. You don't need to say, "Oh gosh, Bob, thank you thank you, thank you! I'm so happy you bought our product. Really, I can't tell you how much I appreciate it."

Such slobbering thanks will leave a bad taste in your client's mouth. He may read it as insincere. He may take it as a sign that you have little faith in your product—you almost sound as if you can't believe someone has finally invested in you.

When you thank your client, stand up straight, shake his hand, and say something like this: "Bob, thank you very much for contracting with Larry's Landscaping. I'm sure you'll be very pleased with the plans we have for your yard."

A verbal thanks, though, can't take the place of a sincerely worded letter.

Write this note as soon as the sale is secure. "Write" is the operative word here.

You should pen the words yourself—not type them out, print them out, or photocopy them.

The more specific the note, the more sincere it sounds, and the better the impression you leave.

Consider the following thank-you note:

> Dear Bob:
>
> Thank you so much for your business.
>
> With Warmest Regards,
> Larry

This note means little to your client. Hastily dashed off, it has the feel of a form letter.

Don't fall into this habit. Instead, take the time to make your personal note as personal as possible. This does not mean you pen an epistle. This does not mean you fawn. It means you succinctly and directly explain why you appreciate a client's business, and how pleased you expect him to be with the results of his contract with you.

> Dear Bob:
>
> I just wanted to take a moment to thank you for contracting with Larry's Landscaping.
>
> I know you interviewed several yard designers before deciding on Larry's, and I truly appreciate your confidence. I'm sure you'll be thrilled with your new garden. The Key West "feel" we discussed will really enhance your property.
>
> I will be in regular contact with you throughout the landscaping process. I'll be popping in on occasion to see how the work is progressing, and I'll also telephone you regularly. Should you ever need to get hold of me,

please don't hesitate to call 555-5555. This is my direct office line. If I'm not here, your call will be automatically transferred to my beeper.

Again, thank you so much for your business. I look forward to working with you.

With Warmest Regards,
Larry

While a written thank-you note should follow every major sale, you can also express your appreciation by other means.

• *E-mails and faxes.* These instant communiqués should never be used as your primary means of thanking a client. They are too quick, too easy, and too informal. If you have just clinched a major sale, the client will appreciate your taking the time to buy a card, pen a personal note, and drive down to the post office to mail it. However, if an existing client provides you with a smaller, or "add-on" sale, electronic thanks are just fine.

Here's an example. In the Larry's Landscaping scenario, Larry has already written Bob a personal thank-you note. As the $10,000 project nears completion, Bob decides that he'd like a $1,000 Jacuzzi set in his tropical garden. After securing a contract for that work, Larry can e-mail or fax Bob a note reading something like this:

Dear Bob:

As per today's conversation, Larry's Landscaping will deliver a Jacuzzi to your home on Thursday, and my workers will install it no later than Monday.

I think this will be a terrific addition to your garden. The Jacuzzi will truly make it the tropical paradise you envisioned.

Thank you so much for your continuing business.

With Warmest Regards,
Larry

- *Thank-you gifts.* After a major sale, you may want to buy your client a gift to express your thanks. Normally, the price of the gift increases with the client's investment. If you sell a car to a writer, you may want to buy her a $30 Cross pen. If you sell a home to an artist, you may want to commission a custom painting of the house's exterior. Beware of gift giving, though: In some instances, especially in the cases of governments or regulated industries, laws may prohibit the practice.

- *Holiday cards.* These serve to both thank your client for his business and keep your name in the forefront of his mind. The preprinted sentiments on these cards should generally be as generic as possible. A holiday card proclaiming "Merry Christmas" may offend any client of a non-Christian faith. You'll find it much safer to use cards that wish clients "A Happy Holiday Season" or "A Joyous New Year."

Your first holiday card to a new client may act much as your original thank-you note. If you have just sold someone a car, for example, your first holiday card may read:

> Dear Phyllis:
>
> Just a short note to thank you for buying that Jaguar this year. I'm sure it will serve you well in the future. Happy New Year!
>
> Sincerely,
> Joe

If several years have passed, and you understand that the client may be itching to buy a new Jaguar, you may want to write:

> Dear Phyllis:
>
> Just a quick note to wish you a happy holiday season. Can you believe that you've already had your Jaguar for six years? You mentioned during our last chat that it still runs very well, but that you're looking for a bigger model. (Kids will do that to you every time.) I'll be calling you

To Gift or Not to Gift?

You own and operate Jacob's Maintenance. A Very Big City has just granted you a $10 million, three-year contract to clean and maintain each of its 75 government buildings.

In appreciation, you purchase a $75,000 Porsche for the mayor.

This is not a thank-you gift. This is a kickback.

While many salespeople give gifts to clients after a major sale or referral, some governments and regulated industries forbid the practice.

Many states, for example, don't allow real estate agents to tip, or provide thank-you gifts, to persons who offer them referrals.

More experienced salespeople in your office may know the rules and customs governing gift giving in your industry. But if they don't, call government public-information offices and ask for guidance. In the case of regulated industries, you may also want to call your state's department of professional regulations.

shortly after the new year to chat about some larger models that are coming out soon.

Sincerely,
Joe

While you clearly always want to take the time to thank the persons to whom you've sold, you also want to express appreciation to anyone who helps you get a sale. This means primarily to satisfied clients who've referred you to prospects.

You should pen these notes immediately after you have clinched a sale. They run something like this:

Dear Bob:

Thank you so much for recommending Larry's Landscaping to your friend Rich Taylor. He's set on a Southwest feel for his yard, and I think it will really enhance the overall look of his property.

I always feel terrific when one of our clients is so satisfied with our work that he refers us to his friends and family members. Thank you so much.

With Warmest Regards,
Larry

You may even feel it appropriate to give your "refer-ee" a gift of thanks. By all means do so, unless prohibited by law or custom.

Taking Care

You've clinched the sale, cashed the check, and gleefully accepted your commission. Think you're finished with this client? Sure. He's a done deal. Write him off. Unless, of course, you want to forge a successful sales career. Then you need to follow up with your customer. Contact him—call or drop by—shortly after your product has been delivered or his use of your service has begun. See if it's working out as he'd

hoped. If not, determine what you can do to make him happy.

Beware, though: Don't ask, "Is everything all right?"

Your prospect will respond with, "Yeah, sure. Fine."

But he may not mean it. He may, in fact, be dissatisfied with your wares. He might not tell you he's annoyed or disappointed, but he'll surely mention it to his friends.

This is how you get a bad rep. You lose referrals and repeat business.

Wouldn't you rather give yourself the chance to make your customer happy?

In chapter 7 we discussed the importance of asking strategic questions during your presentation. Your customer-care questions should prove no less specific.

Consider your own life as a consumer.

Ever gone out for a really fine meal? You felt willing to spend 75 bucks a head because Giovanni's restaurant is said to serve really fine Bordeaux, homemade pasta cooked al dente, escarole with just the right amount of garlic, and a tiramisu creamy enough to make a strong man weep.

Except....

Except the entire meal disappointed you. The Bordeaux had corked, the pasta got cooked to goo, the chef so overloaded the escarole with garlic that you actually feared speaking to your date, and the tiramisu was a sodden lump.

After dinner, Giovanni himself walked onto the floor. He patted your back and asked, "Is everything OK here?"

You responded "Fine."

Don't ask me why people almost always respond "fine." They just do.

Now turn this scenario around. Suppose Giovanni had asked, "Could we have done anything to improve your meal?"

This is an opening you would take. You would say, "The Bordeaux has gone sour. The pasta tasted like glue, the tiramisu was soggy, and as for your escarole, has the chef ever used the words 'garlic' and 'moderation' in the same sentence?"

These may seem like harsh words to you, and they are. But Giovanni has shown you that he cares enough about his restaurant to elicit your true feelings about your meal. And you've done him a favor by speaking the truth. You've given him the opportunity to remedy the situation, and perhaps retain a customer.

He may respond this way: "I'm so sorry to hear you were disappointed with your meal, but I appreciate your honesty. Please give me a chance to make it up to you. Our regular chef came down with the flu, and clearly, the stand-in we hired doesn't meet our usual standards. We'll have to find another. For now, though, I will not charge you for this meal if you promise that you will come back in one week, when our regular chef is working."

You need to phrase follow-up questions in a way that will elicit an honest response. That way, if your client has encountered a problem with your product or service, you will be able to fix it. Your willingness to fix it will impress. It will lead to repeat sales and repeat business.

Never allow a customer to say "fine." Uncover his true concerns.

MAKING *a* Career *in* SALES

CHAPTER ELEVEN

The skills you've learned in this book can get you your first sale. And that's terrific.

You may even close a slew of contracts. And that's better.

But to make a lifetime career in sales—to keep getting up each morning not knowing what the day will bring, to soldier on in the face of inevitable slumps and rejections—takes a combination of skill, attitude, time management, and public relations.

Perhaps the most important of these is attitude—notably, self-confidence.

Beware, though: Unwarranted self-confidence can prove hazardous to your career.

Think of it this way. A novice skier should not expect his self-confidence alone to pro-

pel him down steep, black-diamond slopes, full of moguls and ice. A terrific outlook will not keep his leg unbroken.

Before the skier even thinks of tackling killer slopes, he needs to hone his skills. He first must tone his body and learn how to work the equipment. Then his earned self-confidence will flow naturally and appropriately from his accomplishment.

Similarly, all the confidence in the world will not compensate, for example, for your lack of pre-call planning. If a prospect asks you exactly how your service has helped other companies in the industry, don't expect to smile winningly, say, "I have no clue," and still close the sale.

Your professional self-confidence should, and will, grow from the time you begin sharpening your skills and doing your homework.

Remember:

- Know your stuff. Keep abreast of your company's offerings, industry moves, and changes in your prospect's and client's businesses.

- Prospect, then cold call. You know that sales is a numbers game, and the more prospecting you do, the more sales you'll clinch. Prospect as much as you can. And remember: referrals are far and away the best means of reaching new clients.

- Develop your ability to listen, and ask questions. Whether on the phone or during an in-person presentation, these skills prove invaluable. Keep working on them until effective listening and questioning become second nature.

- Link your product to your prospect's needs. Your prospect doesn't care what you think about your product. And he doesn't want to buy a new widget. He wants to fill a need or solve a problem.

- Market yourself and your wares. Get the word out! Through low-cost and no-cost public relations, through claim-staking and other activities, keep your name in the forefront of the community's mind.

- Don't allow yourself to rust. Keep working on your cold-call, presentation, and closing techniques. Practice in front of the mirror, in front of your family, in front of your friends, in any situation you feel comfortable.

- Manage yourself as a business. As your client base grows, your time will become an extremely valuable commodity. Time management techniques (discussed below) can prove invaluable.

Coping with the Slump

Your hard work has paid off and you're selling like gangbusters. Then it happens: The Slump.

Slumps are inevitable. Some weeks, months, or years, you'll soar at the top of your game. Then, sometimes for specific reasons, sometimes not, your days seem ominously empty.

They say that success breeds success, and this is true. As true is the codicil that failure breeds failure. In sales, inevitable periods of slump can lead to depression. Depression saps your confidence. And lack of confidence shows up, like a scarlet letter, on any salesperson—engendering fear in the prospect. A scared prospect won't invest. And the spiral continues downward.

You have to motivate yourself in times of slump. You have to hold your depression at bay.

Accomplish this, in part, by recognizing this simple fact: Slumps happen. To you, to your boss, to the most successful salesperson in your field. You are not alone.

Accept the inevitability of an occasional slowdown, while at the same time motivating yourself to break out of it.

Here's how:

- Recognize the slump, and the potential for depression.

- Examine your sales technique and see if you need to brush up on any of your skills. (A list of common sales mistakes follows.)

- Believe in yourself.

- Generate the enthusiasm you'll need to soldier on by thinking about what motivates your career: money, prestige, a sense of self-worth, providing for your family, the respect of others in your community.

- Don't get discouraged. Stick to your work plan. If each morning, from nine 'til noon, you make cold calls or set appointments, continue to do so.

- Take care of yourself. Clear out the cobwebs in your head through the most healthful means available. Take a long walk to the shopping center and get yourself a fruit juice. Do some yoga. Spend a day in the country. Get enough sleep.

When your career suffers a slump, you will invariably wonder, "Is it me?"

Maybe not. But then again, maybe.

Slowdowns occur for several reasons. Perhaps few companies in your industry invest in anything during the last quarter of their fiscal years. Perhaps your industry has matured, and you have to scrabble to find new prospect veins.

And perhaps you're making some mistakes.

You've worked hard learning sales skills, but remember: These skills often need reinforcement. The friendly, concerned, and interested cadence of your voice as you make cold calls might, if you're not careful, eventually take on the dead tone of a recorded message. You may have fallen so much in love with your company's latest product that you're giving in to the temptation to talk too much and listen too little during presentations.

Constantly re-examine your technique to see if it's rusty. Here is a list of some common sales mistakes:

- *Talking too much.* Remember, a salesperson needs to carefully listen to and question his prospects to uncover their hidden needs. Only then can he match his product to those needs. No matter how excited you are about a product or service, don't walk in mindlessly blathering about its features.

- *Talking too fast.* Sometimes the fear of "bothering" a prospect or taking up too much of his time can lead you to speak more quickly than you should, and you start to sound like a barker peddling his wares. Nothing will scare a prospect more than the stereotype of the "fast-talking sales-man." Calm down. Decide what you want to say in advance, (you may even want to write a short script at first), then speak at a normal speed.

- *Loss of enthusiasm.* At first, you couldn't believe your good fortune to have landed a job representing such a wonderful product. Then you handle the product day after day, presentation after presentation, and you feel your enthusiasm wane. This is both natural and dangerous. How can you expect a prospect to fall in love with your product if you've fallen out? You can work your way out of this problem in two ways. First, your company will probably keep adding to its line or improve on existing products, giving you a whole new range of options to get excited about. Second, you can generate enthusiasm by thinking about helping new prospects. People—with their infinite array of needs, concerns, and personalities—will never bore you.

- *Nervousness during presentations.* If a prospect has invited you to his office, he has shown his willingness to devote some of his time to you. If he were not interested in what you have to say, he wouldn't have asked you in. Relax. You're welcome here.

- *Lack of planning.* Pre-call planning is an important part of any presentation. Before you walk in, you can find out many of your prospect's needs. Don't skimp on this step.

- *Selling too well, for too long.* While success breeds success, it can also breed complacency. Getting to the top is tough. Staying there is tougher. Don't lose your edge. Keep expanding your client base. And don't forget to follow up with existing clients.

- *Forgetting to ask for referrals.* Some new salesmen feel uncomfortable asking their clients for the "favor" of a referral. This is a fatal mistake, and a needless one. Your new client has invested in your product or service because it fills a need. You've helped him. Now, doesn't he want to help his friends, business associates, or relatives who have the same need? He does them a favor by giving you their contact information.

- *Selling too hard.* You're suffering from a slump and want to break out of it. That's only natural. But because of this, you may naturally begin to push too hard for sales, practically demanding that your prospect invest in your service. Stop it, right now. A "hard sell" will only scare off your prospect and sully your reputation. And that, of course, only prolongs your slump.

Building Your Business

You want to attract as large a clientele as possible, and you want to learn how to manage your time once the clients start rolling in.

As discussed throughout this book, the only way to earn a sound reputation is to represent a reputable product and company, and to conduct yourself reputably. However, don't expect your image as an ethical salesperson alone to propel you to success. You have to develop a name for yourself. This will come, in part, from your standing among clients. However, a little nudge in the publicity department never hurt, either.

Here are some ways to do it:

- Low-cost and no-cost public relations
  A sound public-relations strategy doesn't require hiring a team of image consultants. There are no-cost and low-cost ways to do it yourself. Offer

to write a column on your area of expertise for a local newspaper. Post a Web site. Publish, from your computer, a quarterly industry newsletter and send it to all clients and prospects. Give a free lecture at a local college. Or offer to speak before the regional Chamber of Commerce and any other business, community, or fraternal organization you either claim-stake or believe would have an interest in your wares.

- Advertise
  Does your product have a broad consumer appeal? Is it industry-specific? You've got some thinking to do before you decide where to invest your advertising dollars. While well-placed ads in magazines, or commercials on radio and TV, can prove cost-effective, you want to "prospect" advertising outlets the same way you prospect potential clients. Otherwise, you risk throwing your money away in a vain attempt to speak to the wrong audience. If you represent a rare books dealer, you may want to advertise in *The New Yorker*, but not necessarily in the Yellow Pages. The latter reaches too broad an audience. However, if you sell furniture, your local Yellow Pages may do just fine. Finally, if you represent a product with a broad consumer appeal but only work in a defined geographic area, you may want to advertise in local newspapers or magazines.

- Trade shows
  Selling lumber? Set up a booth at your local homebuilders' show. Representing a television manufacturer? A consumer electronics show will give you important "face time" with a plethora of buyers. Your company itself may set up a booth at these events. If it does not, you may want to invest in one yourself. A "tip" to working these shows: While a number of buyers will naturally just stop by, it's best to target the ones you specifically wish to speak with, and set up specific appointments to meet. Then use the time to show off your wares.

- Networking
  As discussed in chapter 5, you need to be seen. Join and claim-stake as many business, fraternal, social, and community organizations as possible.

Time Management

The harder I work, the further behind I get.

So goes the old joke, anyway. And, too often, so goes the truth.

As your customer base grows, your time will become a far more valuable commodity. You need to manage your tasks—prioritize them, control them—to garner as many sales as possible.

Here's how:

- Set goals for yourself. It's important that you write them down. You need to hold yourself accountable to them, and they're too easy to avoid unless you can repeatedly refer to them, in black and white. Also, make all your aims as specific as possible. Don't simply write, "I want to sell more." Instead, think about how much or to whom you wish to sell. Write, "I want to close four new clients this month." Then name them.

- Prioritize. Determine which of your goals are most important to you, and invest the lion's share of your efforts into achieving them.

- Determine which tasks will help you achieve your goals. Once you've set and prioritized your goals, you need to determine which tasks will best help you achieve them. For example, you may want to close four new clients in a given month, but discover that your prospect file has grown thin. You will want to devote more time to prospecting.

- Record your appointments, and block your time. Never, ever, fail to record an appointment in your calendar. You may think you couldn't possibly forget a presentation appointment but, as you get more busy it does happen. You also have to block out your time to accomplish all the other tasks before you. You're far more likely to actually spend those three hours cold-calling if you block out that time in your calendar, as if it were a firm appointment. You know what tasks you need to complete to achieve your goals. Block out time to complete them.

- Travel efficiently. Consider geography when determining what you want to get accomplished during the week. Here's an example. Suppose you sell washer/dryer combos direct to the consumer, and you want to check out your county registrar's office to see who has filed for marriage licenses. Meanwhile, you have a Tuesday presentation scheduled with a prospect whose office sits just three blocks from the county courthouse. You'll save yourself a lot of time and mileage if you schedule your courthouse time immediately after or prior to your presentation.

- Take the time to plan. Never walk into the office in the morning having no plan for your day. It's best for your morale to hit the morning running. Spend a few minutes at the end of each workday jotting down what you plan to accomplish the following morning. On Fridays, spend a little more time planning what you hope to accomplish during the coming week. Finally, at the end of each month, and each year, plan time to...plan. Sit down and consider what your overall goals are and what tasks you need to perform to achieve these goals. Finally, refer to these goals regularly, determine whether you're on track, and revise them as necessary.

Sales Secrets

In sales, your attitude can win half the battle. To stay motivated, remember these sales secrets:

EXCEPTIONS TO THE TIME-BLOCK RULE

In general, you want to set aside blocks of time for specific chores, and discipline yourself to stick to the schedule.

If you set aside three hours for cold calling each Monday afternoon, make sure you actually spend that time dialing. Consider this no less a commitment than a scheduled presentation appointment.

However, there are exceptions to every rule—notably when it comes to customer care.

Interrupt your scheduled tasks to return queries from existing clients. They're financially supporting you with their business, and providing you veins of qualified leads through referrals.

Always place existing customers before prospects.

Sales Ratios You Need to Know

How many presentations does it take for you to get a single sale? How many cold calls does it take for you to get an appointment? How many of your referrals are actually qualified? How many hours do you work for the money you earn?

You need to keep track of these ratios.

Here's why.

Suppose you start with a presentation-to-sale ratio of 1 to 10. (One sale closed per every 10 appointments.) As the months go buy, you notice that the ratio increases to 1 to 7, then 1 to 5. This should occur naturally, as you hone your presentation skills.

Then, after a year or so, you notice that you're back down to 1 to 10.

This drop may indicate that something is wrong with your technique. Have you lost enthusiasm for your product? Have you given the same presentation so many times that you're starting to sound like a robot? Do so many of your prospects have the same needs that you've begun to assume you know what every new contract truly wants?

Keep track of these ratios. If you notice your cold-call-to-appointment ratio beginning to slip, determine whether you're making mistakes in that area (talking too fast, being too long-winded). If your referrals aren't panning out the way they used to, you may need to think about whether you're helping clients narrow down the enormous number of people each knows to the few who truly need your product or service. And if you keep working longer and longer hours for the same or smaller return, you may need to better organize your time.

Babe Ruth Was the Strikeout King

Babe Ruth struck out. A lot. He batted "only" a .376. Still, baseball fans revere him as one of the greatest athletes to ever grace the game.

Baseball is a game built on numbers and ratios. So is your sales career. You will strike out a lot. You will never bat 1,000. The more at-bats you take—cold calls, presentations—the more often you will strike out. But the more sales you'll make.

Think of the old proverb, "He who never falls as rarely climbs."

Gandhi Didn't Eat Cheeseburgers

You don't have to sell to everyone. You don't want to sell to everyone. You represent a specific product or service, and only a certain portion of the population will have a need for it. A diaper salesperson doesn't want to meet with couples blissfully childless. You'll only waste your time and energy. And your spirits will flag in the process.

Instead, spend your time prospecting—devising lists of people who you truly believe have a need or a desire for your product. Your call-to-sales ratios will run much better, you will spend your time more efficiently, and your confidence will soar.

It Takes Years to Become an Overnight Success

The long-term view is the only view. It takes years to become an overnight success.

Suppose you represent an interior-design firm and have claim-staked your local Chamber of Commerce. You are one of three interior designers in the organization, and your fellow chamber members keep turning to the other two. For a year, they only call on the other two.

What's wrong with you?

You get absolutely nothing. Except maybe for this: You're new. You've yet to develop a name. You've yet to earn a track record that prospects trust.

You build that track record—one client at a time.

The Ruby Slippers Always Worked

You cannot expect others to believe in your product if you don't believe in it yourself. You cannot expect prospects to trust your company if you have any doubts about its business practices.

Your distrust will quickly lead to prospects' distrust.

Affiliate yourself with a product that you think is dynamite. And make sure that product is sold by an ethical company.

Go for the "No"

Never leave a presentation with a prospect promising nothing more than to "think about" your offer.

As a rule, "I'll think about it" means "no." Your head knows that, but your heart won't want to believe it.

If a prospect has promised to think about your offer, you'll go home and try to figure out ways to get him to a yes. But at this late date, you're likely wasting your time.

Get the prospect to commit to something—to a close, to advancement, or even to a no—before you end your presentation. Any type of firm statement leads you to an action plan. And a plan of action, even if it's just writing off this particular sale, is better for your attitude than mental dithering.

No One Ever Got Rich Lowering His Prices

Offer price breaks to your prospects sparingly, if at all. Don't eat into your company's margins or your own commission every time a prospect starts to dither. Rather, spend some more time helping your prospect understand a product's value by directly linking it to his needs.

WII-FM: Everyone's Favorite Station

All prospects eye purchases thinking, "What's in it for me?" They may want something to fill a business need, or they may want a luxury item that will accomplish little more than making them feel good or perhaps enhance their status in the community. Finding "something in it for me" turns prospects into clients.

If it's important to your client, it's important. Period. End of story.

You sell diamonds and fine costume jewelry. A customer walks in, says she has $2,000 to spend on a glittering stone. She doesn't, however, want an exquisite, 1-carat diamond. It's too small. She wants a 40-carat cubic zirconia.

You may think this choice is ridiculous. But the size is more important to your prospect than the rarity of the stone, its color, cut, or clarity.

Listen to your prospect. Find out what he wants or needs. That's important. What you think is special about your product is not what matters.

Garbage In, Garbage Out

What happens if you spend a lot of time prospecting and virtually no time in pre-call planning? Or what if you spend time on a flawless pre-call plan, then walk into the presentation and start babbling away about the features of your product without taking the time to uncover your prospect's needs?

You lose sales.

As discussed in chapter 2, all sales follow a certain formula: obtain knowledge, prospect, find the Yes Guy, get an appointment, plan your presentation, present your goods, close, generate referrals, and follow up. No one step in this equation is more important than another. Don't think you can blow off a step and still clinch a sale.

Garbage in, garbage out. Sound work in, sales out.

Lose the Gimmicks

Trick sales. Scare tactics. The hard sell.

Forget 'em. They just don't work anymore. As all types of consumers become more sophisticated, sales stunts fall by the wayside. The prospect recognizes them for what they are.

You can only build a successful sales career with quality and persistence. No gimmicks allowed.

Manage Yourself Like a Business

Whether you're a free agent or a member of the sales team, you have to manage yourself as if you were the owner of a business. Depend on no one else to build your client list, manage your time, or publicize your activities. This fact may seem more apparent to small-business owners acting as their own salesmen, and to free agents, than it does to members of a large sales force. But even if you work on a sales force, remember this: The guys at the top get the glory, the money, and the prestige. The guy with the lowest sales gets...fired.

THE Sale

CHAPTER TWELVE

Reading this book, you've learned the techniques you need to use in every step of the sales process, from prospecting to customer care.

Look through the following scenario to see how they all pan out. Beware, though: This story covers only a very simple sale. Not all your work will flow this smoothly.

In the Beginning

Jack Taylor recently graduated from Brown University, with a major in business. He returned home clueless as to what he wanted to do with his life. So he started thinking about the things he enjoys: he likes people, likes to help them, and considers himself an armchair psychologist. He likes research. He likes challenge and variety. He likes to show off a little. And he likes money a lot.

Slowly the idea dawns that he might enjoy sales. He buys several books on the subject. And the more he learns, the more a salesman's life appeals to him. But all the books stress that anyone who wants to forge a successful sales career must absolutely adore the product or service he represents. A prospect can't fall in love with a product if the sales guy hasn't.

Jack sits back and tries to think about what stirs his passions. The healthful life. Feeling good. Eating right. Exercise. Biking in the mountains. The environmental movement. The war against tobacco.

"Terrific," he thinks to himself. "What am I gonna do? Sell mountain bikes at retail? I'm not sure I want to spend my days cooped up in a store. And I don't really think I'm gonna be driving a new Jeep soon, with a job like that."

But he does think that there might be a sales job out there, somewhere, that would both bring him the money, variety, and challenge he wants and promote the healthful life he embraces.

Jack visits his local library, and, using a computerized database of stories appearing in local newspapers, conducts a search of the words "business + environment + health." And 10 stories appear. Several catch his interest, but he especially likes the business profile written about Breathe Easy, Inc., a manufacturer of home and business air-purification systems.

In the article, owner Jan Saperstein waxes poetic about the need for clean air in the home and at work. She talks about how Breathe Easy has become the most successful manufacturer of air-purification systems in the region.

Finally, she talks about the very real hazards inherent in indoor air pollution. Benzene, found in new paints, is believed to cause everything from headaches to cancer; ammonia in cleaning supplies to cause eye irritation and sinus infection; chloroform in paint to cause dizziness; formaldehyde in tobacco smoke to cause depression and cancer; trichlorethylene in glues to cause respiratory irritation. The list goes on.

The reporter's tone indicates that he respects Saperstein's products. He ends this story with the words, "As long as people continue to care for their health, Jan Saperstein will find buyers for her goods."

"Bingo!" thinks Jack, heading out to the pay phone to call Saperstein. She explains to him that Breathe Easy has already hired enough direct-to-consumer salespeople, and now plans to concentrate on to-business sales. Jack touts his Brown business degree, and Saperstein invites him in for an interview.

Jack gets a sales job, with a territory covering institutions and businesses within a 75-mile radius.

The First Day

BZZZ! BZZZ! BZZZZ! An alarm clock wakes Jack at 6:30 in the morning. Having read a lot of sales books, he knows that the proper sales attitude must begin now, even before he has his first cup of coffee.

This is what he says to himself:

"I believe I can help every prospect upon whom I call. I've done my research, and I'm not contacting anyone willy-nilly. These are people who truly need my service, and I'm going to do my best to help them."

He shows up at the office, greets his colleagues. Then the work starts.

While the company has no formal sales-training program, Saperstein is eager to fill him in on the features of the Breathe Easy products, and encourages his own study. Within his first few hours on the job, Jack:

- Talks to his boss about the features of the service: the available delivery schedules, prices, and room-size penetration. He also learns about his territory. Believing that adults often care more for their children's health than their own, Saperstein wants Jack to concentrate on selling to day-care centers within a 75-mile radius, with an eye toward eventually working with schools and children's hospitals. He asks Saperstein if Breathe Easy has already contracted with any day-care operations, and Saperstein notes that she has closed two sales herself, with Building Blocks and Learning Land.

Jack then probes his new boss about Breathe Easy's competition. She relates that no

other air-purification manufacturer operates in the general area, and many of her existing clients appreciate doing business with a local operation. They like being able to call on someone nearby should they experience a problem with the system or need an upgrade.

- Sits down to read the company's product brochures.

- Peruses corporate press releases and advertising. He learns that the company positions itself as a health tool in its print ads with its logo—pictures of smiling, happy families chatting in their homes and a graphic of one of the company's air-purification systems sucking out of the air cartoon-styled pollutants.

- Looks over news articles written about the company.

- Reads and photocopies all the magazine articles the company has collected detailing the environmental hazards of indoor pollutants.

- Goes online to access some magazines covering the day-care industry.

Now it's time to start prospecting, and Jack feels willing to devote quite some time to the task. Since Breathe Easy has just branched out into day-care sales, there are no immediate leads to be found in the office. He'll have to do it all on his own.

But Jack realizes he'll have an easier time prospecting than many other salespeople. Day-care centers in his state must be licensed, and those licenses kept on view in the county in which the centers operate. Grabbing a cup of coffee, he heads to his car, drives over to the county courthouse, finds the department of professional regulations, and asks to see its day-care license registry.

He had no idea this prospect vein would prove so fertile. Literally hundreds of day-care operations, from in-home businesses to large corporate operations to traditional, stand alone set ups, operate in this county alone. And this county represents slightly less than half of his geographic territory. Each license lists the name of the state-approved operator, the name, address, and phone number of his business, and the number of children it can legally handle.

Jack asks for a photocopy of this registry, and heads back to the office. He begins to sort through the listings, a triage of sorts, figuring out which prospects he wants to target first. He sets aside, for now, the tiny in-home operations (too low a commission potential) and day-care operations sponsored by large businesses for their employees—he doesn't yet feel quite up to the challenge of selling through the corporate maze.

That leaves traditional day-care settings. He picks twenty of the largest, and starts calling. He uses a bit of subtle subterfuge to garner some preliminary information about these businesses—notably, which day-care centers may have already bought air-purification systems. Jack doesn't mind trying to upgrade their current systems to Breathe Easy's offerings, but he wants to know what he's up against.

Finally, he needs to find the true Yes Guy. While the licensed operators listed in his registry seem like a great place to start, he's not sure that every licensed operator makes the purchasing decisions for his company.

He starts calling around. His conversations run something like this:

> *Receptionist:* "Good afternoon, Alpha Day Care."
>
> *Jack:* "Good afternoon. My name is Jack, and I need some information about Alpha. I was wondering if you could help me, please?"

(Jack does not identify himself as a salesman. The receptionist at this point probably thinks he's a parent interested in placing a child—and that's fine.)

> *Receptionist:* "I'll sure try."
>
> *Jack:* "Thanks! Could you please tell me how many kids you take care of overall?"
>
> *Receptionist:* "About 150. We have nine separate care rooms."
>
> *Jack:* "And what ages do you accept?
>
> *Receptionist:* "We have specific programs designed for everyone from infants to pre-teens. You should really stop by to get a feel for the place."
>
> *Jack:* "I sure will. Let me ask, do you take sick kids?"

Receptionist: "It depends on the situation. If the child has a communicable illness, we just can't—we have to worry about everyone's health. So, unfortunately, even if your child just has a cold, you'll have to make alternative arrangements until he recovers."

Jack: "I understand. Just one more question: Do you folks have air-purification systems in place?"

Receptionist: "No, uh-uh. But we do make sure all our kids get lots of fresh air, and we open the windows as soon as spring comes. Why do you ask?"

Jack: "Well, you know, there are indoor pollutants that can make kids sick."

Receptionist: "Oh."

Jack: "If I wanted to talk to someone at Alpha about the air-purification situation before making any further decisions, who would that be?"

Receptionist: "Our owner, Kate Montgomery."

Jack: "Thanks an awful lot for your time today."

Jack makes 19 similar calls, then goes home for the night.

The Cold Calls

Bubbling with confidence after a good first day's work, Jack gets to the office quite early the following morning. He knows the best time to try to get Yes Guys is early in the morning, at lunch, or after business hours. Jack is taking the morning route: He wants to hit the day running.

He calls Alpha again, and asks for Kate Montgomery's office. He had hoped to avoid her gatekeeper altogether, but no such luck.

Instead, a secretary answers the phone:

Secretary: "Ms. Montgomery's office, Alice White speaking."

Jack: "Hello, Ms. White. This is Jack Taylor calling from Breathe Easy. Is Kate available, please?"

Secretary: "Can I ask what this is in reference to?"

Jack: "Sure. I'd like to talk to her about reducing colds and sinus infections among Alpha kids."

Secretary: "And you said your name was?"

Jack: "Jack Taylor with Breathe Easy."

Secretary: "Will you hold the line for a moment please, sir? Let me see if Ms. Montgomery is available."

Jack's heart thumps. He has tried to pre-sell the gatekeeper by framing his intro in a way that virtually prohibits her from not putting him through to Kate Montgomery. How could Alice not care about the health of Alpha's little-kid clients?

The tactic works. Soon, he hears a new voice on the other end of the line.

Kate: "Kate Montgomery."

Jack: "Good morning, Ms. Montgomery. This is Jack Taylor calling from Breathe Easy Air Purification. I understand that Alpha currently doesn't have any air-purification systems. Is that correct?"

Kate: "Sure is. I don't think we need any. The building has great ventilation."

Jack: "I understand. I'd like to speak with you about that. Do you have a minute?"

Kate: "One, just one."

Jack: "I promise this will only take a moment. Ms. Montgomery, no matter how well a building is ventilated, no matter how clean it is, air pollutants can cause severe colds and sinus problems among its occupants, especially children. I'd like to stop by your office for about a half-hour this week, to explain our program."

Kate: "No, I don't think so. I mean, I'm certainly concerned about the health of our kids, that's why I had a great ventilation system installed. On top of that, we open all the windows in the building as soon as it gets warm enough, and we keep the place very clean."

Jack: "I'm sure you do. Alpha has a great reputation. But, ma'am, are you aware that even the ammonia in certain cleaning products can cause respiratory and sinus infections?"

Kate: "No. No, I didn't know that."

Jack: "Don't worry. Most people don't. But if you don't mind my saying so, perhaps you need to be especially concerned. Little kids are more susceptible to pollutants than grown-ups are, and you, of course, want Alpha's kids to be healthy and happy. Also, when the kids do come down with colds, you, understandably, can't accept them. Investing in an air-purification system can actually help save you money, in terms of reduced absenteeism. Everybody likes to save money, don't they?"

Kate: "Yeah. Saving money is good."

Jack: "Great. Ms. Montgomery, what would be a better day for our meeting? Tuesday or Thursday?"

Kate: "I guess I could spare twenty minutes or so on Thursday afternoon. The later the better."

Jack: "Would you prefer 4 or 4:30?"

Kate: "4:30."

Jack: "Terrific. Ms. Montgomery, I'll see you at 4:30 on Thursday. Thanks a lot for your time, and I look forward to meeting you."

Kate: "See you then."

Jack hangs up the phone, grinning. He's in.

Prep Work

Jack now has to prepare for his meeting with Kate Montgomery. He runs over to the library, accessing its electronic databases of local and regional magazines, pulling up every article he can on Alpha. One business-magazine profile describes Alpha as one of the most popular day-care centers in the area, and notes that Montgomery plans to open a second location within the next two years. Her child-care techniques follow the Montessori method, and she seems to have an environmental bent: Every year on Arbor Day, she and her employees round up the older kids, take them to a local park, and plant several trees. On the way back to the office, Jack buzzes by Alpha and asks the receptionist for some brochures. While there, he takes in the overall ambiance of the building. It boasts a cheerful, homey feel.

Back at the office, he draws up a detailed similar-situation scenario covering how Breathe Easy helped Building Blocks save money by improving the health of its clients. Since his boss, Jan Saperstein, closed that sale, he gets some of his info from her. He also asks her to call the Building Blocks president, to see if he can use her as a reference. Jan gets the OK. He prepares an order form for Alpha.

Then he returns to his cold calls, putting his nose to the grindstone. He's excited about Thursday.

In the Door

Jack arrives at Alpha Day Care at 4:20. He introduces himself and takes in the surroundings some more, until the receptionist escorts him to Kate Montgomery's office.

He cuts a nice figure as he walks in. Wearing a well-tailored suit and freshly shined shoes, he smiles at Kate as she stands. He looks her in the eye, shakes her hand firmly—but not too firmly—and waits for her to offer him a seat.

Then the two begin to talk, with Jack employing strategic questions.

> *Jack:* "Kate, I'd like to thank you for taking the time to meet with me today."
>
> *Kate:* "My pleasure."
>
> *Jack:* "As I mentioned during our telephone conversation, Breathe Easy has been able to help several businesses like yours, including Building Blocks, reduce their absenteeism by improving the health of their clients. But before we get into that, I'd like to learn a little bit more about your business. Can you please tell me about your clientele? I know that Alpha has a glowing reputation, but what specifically makes parents place their kids here, do you think?"
>
> *Kate:* "Well, I'd say the Montessori method is a big draw. More and more

parents, it seems, appreciate the fact that kids learn by doing. They also appreciate the patience, and the firmness, of our staff. We never, ever, yell at children. We're very loving, but we do set boundaries. I truly believe that kids need structure, and limits. They practically cry for it. We have a very high staff-to-client ratio and I think our parents also appreciate that. No child lacks attention here. Finally, I know this is something of a dirty word these days, but—go ahead—label me. I'm politically correct. Our toys, our books. We try to represent as many different races, and as many different lifestyles as possible. This is a real socially conscious town, and I think our parents appreciate this approach."

Jack: "I see. Tell me a little more about the forms your social consciousness takes."

Kate: "Sure. You know, during the summer, when school is out, we have kids here as old as ten. We do a lot of field trips with them. Some of them are strictly for fun—some local amusement parks, hikes in the woods. Others are a little more serious. We put together some plays, and perform them at local nursing homes, we plant trees in local parks, that type of thing."

Jack: "Wow, that sounds like a wonderful program. Let me ask you—so far, you've mentioned hikes with the kids and planting trees. Do you think your clients' social consciousness extends to the environment?"

Kate (laughing): "I think I see where you're headed with this. And yes, it does. And yes, they're probably more concerned about their kids' indoor environment than they are about the outdoor environment."

Jack (laughing): "OK. You caught me. Let me ask you, though, why have you not yet invested in an air-purification system?"

Kate: "Before talking with you, I never even considered the idea, so I'd guess you'd say ignorance, mostly. But now I've done some research on indoor air pollutants, and frankly the information I found scared me a little. Purifiers are a good idea, but I worry about the cost. Our parents pay a fairly high rate to place their kids here, and we just had a price increase at the New Year. I don't want to pass any new charges onto them."

Jack: "Sure. Kate, if I understand correctly, you like the health benefits of an air-purification system, but you don't want your overhead expenses to rise, is that correct?"

Kate: "Exactly, yes."

Jack: "Kate, Breathe Easy will be able to help. First, all our air purifiers filter indoor pollutants, including benzene, ammonia, chloroform, formaldehyde, and trichlorethylene. Second, because these pollutants are known to cause disease and infection, having purifiers will help keep Alpha's kids healthy, and you'll see reduced losses due to sick days. Let me ask you, what does it cost to place kids here?"

Kate: "One hundred dollars per week, or twenty dollars a day."

Jack: "And you don't charge for days when kids get sick, and you can't care for them, isn't that right?"

Kate: "That's right. At the end of the month, we refund parents for any days their children have missed because of illness.

Jack: "How many absences do you see each day?"

Kate: "On average, four to five."

Jack: "OK. Let's take four on average. That's $80 per day. Uh, Kate...do you mind if I move my chair over, so you and I can do some math together?"

Kate: "Not at all."

Jack and Kate now sit on the same side of the desk.

Jack: "OK. You lose eighty dollars a day to absenteeism, or $400 per week, isn't that right?"

Kate: "Yes."

Jack: "OK. And $400 per week times 52 weeks equals $20,800 per year, isn't that right?"

Kate: "Yup. It's a large chunk of change for us."

Jack: "Kate, Breathe Easy can install air purifiers in each of your nine care rooms, your reception area, and your office, for a total of $11,000. Now,

if even a quarter of your absenteeism is caused, or aggravated, by children's contacts with pollution, you'll save $5,400 per year, and the purifiers will pay for themselves in two years. Now, since these purifiers come with a ten-year warranty, you'll have at least seven years of actually making money—the purifiers will have been paid for, and you'll continue to see the benefits of reduced absenteeism."

Kate: "I have to admit, this looks really impressive."

Jack (removing from his briefcase an order form already filled out): "Terrific! When would you prefer we start installation, Monday or the following week?"

Kate: "No, I'm not ready for that, yet. I'm just not sure."

Jack: "I understand that this is a big decision for you, Kate, but let me ask—What are you unsure about? Is there something I've not explained clearly?"

Kate: "No, no, I understand everything you've said. It's just that. Well...how do I know how many childhood illness are actually caused by indoor pollutants? Suppose I spend the 11 grand, and my absenteeism doesn't fall at all?"

Jack: "Kate, I'm not going to lie to you. Medical science estimates that a large portion of childhood ailments are caused or exacerbated by indoor pollution, but there's no way I can give you an exact percentage. What I can do is show you what our products have done to reduce absenteeism at other day-care centers. *(He removes from his briefcase a similar-situation scenario.)* Take a look at this. As you can see, Building Blocks day care has seen a 29 percent reduction in absenteeism since installing our products."

Kate (looking over the scenario): "Twenty-nine percent? Are you sure?"

Jack: "Would you like us to call Building Blocks? The owner over there, Martha McGuire, said she'd be happy to speak with you."

Kate: "You know what, that's all right."

Jack: "Great. So would you prefer we begin installation this Monday or the following week?"

Kate: "This Monday would be great."

Jack smiles. He's just clinched his first sale. He knows that there will be lots of follow-up work and customer care in the future. But for now, he's pleased as punch. And, after Kate signs the contracts, he remembers there's one more piece of work to be done today. Here. Now.

Jack: "Kate, I really appreciate your business. I'm sure you'll be pleased with Breathe Easy."

Kate: "No, thank *you*. A lot. I feel good about this decision. I mean, savings issues aside, I'm in the business of caring for kids. I sure don't want to contribute to making them sick."

Jack: "Hey, that's what I'm here for. Kate, just before I go, I wonder if there's one more thing you can help me with?"

Kate: "I'll try."

Jack: "I'm trying hard to build up Breathe Easy's business in this county, and in neighboring ones. I was wondering whether you knew of any other day-care providers who might have a need for our products? Day-care owners who are as concerned as you about the health of the kids they care for?"

Kate: "Well, I have to tell you, I'm not as "up" as I should be on what all my competitors are doing. But I'm pretty good friends with Charlotte Kinter, who owns Bo Peep Day Care over on 7th Street. She and I did a lot of environmental work together in the early 70s, and she's really into the health movement. Oh! And Tom Glaser, a dear friend of mine, is going to open a day-care center next year, specifically geared to physically and mentally challenged children. If all these indoor pollutants can make even healthy kids sick, I'd hate to think what they can do to kids with serious medical conditions."

Jack: "That was Tom Glaser, you said?"

Kate: "Yeah. G-l-a-s-e-r."

Jack: "Do you have a phone number for him?"

Kate: "Sure. It's 555-1111. He lives over on Fourth Street."

Jack: "Kate, I really appreciate your help."

One sale does not a career make, but Jack's off to a good start. He has learned the mechanics of selling, from attitude and prospecting to closing and customer care, and sharpened his techniques along the way. His first closing sets the foundation for a challenging, lifelong occupation. The road may not always, as they say, prove smooth. But at least he's got a clue.

GLOSSARY

advancement: Any step taken that brings you closer to an actual sale, such as the step from cold calling to a face–to–face presentation, the step from face–to–face presentation to answering a prospect's objections, the step from answering objections to closing.

balance sheet: A closing technique that entails you helping a prospect list, on one side of a sheet of paper, all the positive aspects of investment in your product or service. You then allow the prospect to list, for himself, all its drawbacks.

boards of directors: The corporate governing boards that often hold ultimate buying power in an organization. These entities many times simply rubber–stamp decisions already made by their employees.

body language: These nonverbal signals serve as a means of communication between the prospect/client and you. Understand your prospect's body language—sitting forward to indicate interest, tapping his feet to indicate impatience or anxiety—and move your presentation appropriately.

broad questions: Questions posed by you to garner general information about a prospect or her business.

choice of alternatives: A closing technique whereby you offer your prospect a choice between two or more products or services.

claim-staking: Joining as many business, social, community, church, or fraternal organizations as possible to find qualified leads.

client/customer: Someone who has already purchased goods from your company.

closes: Techniques that lead the customer to buy your product or service.

closing: The process of getting a prospect to buy your goods.

cold calling: Telephoning a prospect with the aim of securing a face–to–face meeting for your presentation.

commission: The money you earn for each sale completed. The amount is usually a percentage of the product's sale price.

competition: Those corporations that vie with you to reach the same clientele.

competition knowledge: Your understanding of the competition's position in the market, and their business strengths and weaknesses.

corporate surroundings: The decor of an office and demeanor of its employees. Corporate surroundings are an indication of a business's culture, and often, in smaller operations, the personality of its president.

cost: The amount of money your corporation charges for its product or service. See Value.

customer care: Following up with a client after you've closed a sale to ensure that your product or service is working correctly. Customer care practices help garner repeat business.

dumped customers: Clients of salespeople who used to work for your employer, but who have since quit or retired, or been laid off. These clients can often serve as qualified leads for you.

fear: The primary stumbling block preventing a prospect from purchasing a product or service. Prospects have an inherent fear of saying yes to any major purchase. You help them to overcome that fear.

first impression: The first thoughts of you, your company, or product that cross through a prospect's mind.

focus questions: Questions posed by you to a prospect to uncover her hidden needs. These questions help you link your product to as many of the prospect's concerns as possible.

gatekeepers: Secretaries, executive assistants, security guards, voice-mail systems and any other barrier that keeps you from speaking directly to the Yes Guy.

hidden features: These secondary offerings of your product or service may help you sell to those prospects who sit on the "should I buy?" fence. Hidden features include warranties, delivery schedules, product support, and money–back guarantees.

hidden needs: A prospect's secondary desire for a product.

hot buttons: Statements made by a salesman to grab the prospect's interest.

industry lingo: The jargon used by workers in any business field. A working knowledge of your client's lingo can help convince him that you are a true industry insider.

industry knowledge: Your understanding of the industry in which you work, and how changes in that industry may affect your prospect or client.

itch cycles: Known buying cycles. These can be based on life cycles of a given product, or customer trends toward replacement/buy ups.

linking: Matching your product or service as closely as possible to your prospect's needs.

long-term view: The process of planning today and working toward a long–term sales career.

marketing: Positioning your product, through advertising and public relations strategies, in the public mind-set.

multiple choice question: Giving a prospect a choice between the purchase of Product A or Product B.

natural-born salesman: A pervasive myth holding that certain persons can forge successful sales careers through the strength of their personalities alone.

networking: Increasing your circle of associates, friends, and business contacts by joining fraternal, social, and community organizations. This will help you generate qualified leads. See Claim–staking.

no guy: People in a social unit, family, or business who are incapable of saying yes to your proposal—often because they don't boast the buying power. Salesmen too often waste their time trying to sell to the No Guy.

objections: All the reasons a prospect gives you for not buying your product or service.

obligating questions: An aid toward advancing or closing the sale. Obligating questions constitute a promise made if the prospect agrees to buy.

obligating close: A closing technique entailing the use of Obligating Questions.

obvious users: Prospects who have a clear need for your product or service. If you sell dog food to consumers, your local kennel club is a group of obvious users.

presentation/demonstration: A face-to-face meeting with the Yes Guy through which you try to secure a contract for your product or service.

porcupine: The practice of answering a prospect's questions with questions, to better understand a prospect's concerns about the product or service offered.

position: A product's niche in the popular mind-set, usually developed through advertising and public-relations efforts.

positive emotions: Enthusiasm, want, and the like. Successful salespeople are able to help prospects supplant their fear of buying with positive emotions of ownership.

pre–call planning: Research done after having garnered a presentation appointment to determine what a company's true needs are.

product knowledge: Your understanding of the product or service you represent.

proprietary information: Specific information about the companies or consumers you serve. Proprietary information can include a company's gross earnings, number of clients, or names of clients. As a reputable salesperson, you never share a client's proprietary information with anyone else unless you have been given permission to do so.

prospect: A qualified lead.

prospecting: The act of generating qualified leads.

puppy dog: A closing technique where you help your prospect decide to buy by allowing him a free trial of a product or service.

purchasing departments: Departments of large businesses responsible for buying the day–to–day materials needed to keep the organization running smoothly. Depending on the business or service you represent, the purchasing department may or may not be the home of your Yes Guy.

qualified leads: People or companies that you know have both a legitimate need for your offering and the cash to pay for it.

references: Current clients who will recommend you, your company, and your product to a prospect.

reference persons: Persons to whom others turn for information. Part of your job as a salesperson is to become an expert about your community or industry so as to serve as a reference person to your clients.

referrals: Qualified leads given to you by a satisfied customer. Referrals are the best way to get new clients.

reverse directories: Telephone directories that list phone numbers by street and area. They are helpful in targeting a given section of town.

sales aids: Brochures, literature, and products that help keep your prospect involved in a presentation, and therefore help you advance the sale.

sales monologues: This ineffective presentation technique entails a salesperson beginning a presentation with a long speech about his product or service, without first asking strategic questions to uncover the prospect's needs.

sales ratios: Percentages you need to track, including the number of cold calls made to presentations garnered, the number of presentations made to closes, and the number of hours worked to money earned.

self-talk: The unconscious way in which we communicate with ourselves. What a salesperson tells herself contributes greatly to her mind-set. Keep all your self–talk positive. Believe in your ability to help a prospect or client.

SIC codes: Codes developed by the Securities and Exchange Commission to track businesses by industry. Can prove extremely helpful to those who work in industry-wide sales.

similar-situation close: Closing by recalling for the prospect how you have helped other clients facing similar issues.

similar-situation scenarios: Stories of how you've helped other clients, used to encourage a current prospect to buy.

slump: A time of slow business activity.

smokestacking: Visiting local business and industrial parks to see who has set up shop there, and to determine if any of these companies have a likely use for your product or service.

solution: A product or service that satisfies the needs of the prospect.

tie downs: Statements that the salesperson turns into questions to engender a conversational feel during his discussions with prospects and clients.

time management: The process of organizing and grouping your work tasks to use your business hours most efficiently.

value: A prospect's perceived worth of your product or service.

value questions: Questions you pose to determine what type of worth a prospect places on a product or service. This loosely translates into what the prospect is willing to pay for it.

World Wide Web pages: Pages posted by corporations on the Internet for public view. You can use these to help determine the needs of your prospects.

Yes Guy: The person in an organization or family unit who has both the desire for your goods and the means to pay for it.

yes or no questions: The most inefficient type of query around, it entails asking a prospect a question which can only be answered with a yes or a no.

RESOURCES

Books

Seth Godin, *If You're Clueless about Starting Your Own Business and Want to Know More* (Chicago:Upstart Publishing Company, 1998).

Tom Hopkins, *How to Master the Art of Selling* (Scottsdale, AZ: Warner Books/Champion Press, 1994).

Nicki Joy with Susan Kane-Benson, *Selling Is a Woman's Game* (New York: Avon Books, 1994).

Guy Kawasaki, *Selling the Dream* (New York: HarperCollins Publishers, 1992).

Lawrence Kohn and Joel Saltzman, *Selling with Honor* (New York: The Berkeley Publishing Group, 1997).

Jay Conrad Levinson, Bill Gallagher, et al., *Guerrilla Selling* (New York: Houghton Mifflin, 1992).

Michael T. McGaulley, *Selling 101* (Holbrook, MA: Adams Media Corporation, 1997).

Barry Masser and William Leeds, *Power Selling by Telephone* (Englewood Cliffs, NJ: Prentice Hall, 1983).

Robert B. Miller and Stephen E. Heiman with Tad Tuleja, *Conceptual Selling* (New York: Warner, 1989).

Anthony Parinello, *Selling to Vito: The Very Important Top Officer* (Holbrook, MA: Adams Media Corp., 1994).

David Peoples, *Selling to the Top* (New York: John Wiley & Sons, 1993).

Don Peppers, *Life's a Pitch and Then You Buy* (New York: Currency/Doubleday, 1995).

Tom Reily, *Value-Added Selling Techniques—How to Sell More Profitably, Confidently, and Professionally* (Chicago: Congdon & Weed, 1989).

Nancy J. Stephens with Bob Adams, *Customer-Focused Selling* (Adams Media Corporation, Holbrook, MA: 1997).

Online Resources

GCN Consultants Web site: www.interlog.com/~gcn

Sales Doctors Magazine Web site: http://salesdoctors.com

Entrepreneurial Edge Magazine Web site: http://www.edgeonline.com

The Electric Library: http://www3.elibrary.com

The SEC Web site: http://www.sec.gov

Magazine and Newspaper Articles

"Believe It Or Not: Most Highly Successful Sales People are Highly Ethical." Business Wire, http://www.businesswire.com, 1998.

"Working from Home: Don't Buy Into the Idea that Selling is Hard." The Los Angeles Times, P.O. Box 7032, Torrance, CA 90504. 1998.

"Selling May Look Easy, But It Takes Some Skill." Newsday, 235 Pinelawn Road, Melville, NY 11747. 1998.